Backcasts

About The Author

John Knowles moved from Florida to Detroit in 1926 to work for the *Detroit Free Press*. In 1940, he joined a major oil company and worked there until his retirement in 1965 as Vice President. The woods and streams have always been John's favorite playground and fly fishing his love. He has fished with the best—John Voelker, Paul Young, George Mason, Lyle Dickerson, Mike Cavanagh, Ray Bergman, and many others.

As a Lt. Col in the 10th Air Force, his love of flying led to owning and operating an aircraft service in Detroit as a sideline for many years. John now resides with his wife Margie in Bath, Michigan.

Backcasts

Memories And Recollections
Of Seventy Years
As A Sportsman

Fishing, Hunting
And Other Stories

John Knowles

Wilderness Adventure Books
320 Garden Lane
P.O. Box 968
Fowlerville, Michigan 48836

Manufactured in the United States of America

Table Of Contents

Preface

Recently, I was invited to be a guest speaker at a Trout Unlimited meeting in Lansing, Michigan. I had never done anything like that before and I was reluctant to do so. But, I was a last resort for them so I agreed to talk about something that would be of interest to the group. I stood up in front of that gang of sportsmen and talked for an hour off the cuff. Mostly about fly fishing and about the many things that happened to me during my seventy years as a fisherman and a hunter.

After the meeting, several people came over to me and shook my hand and told me what a wonderful talk I had given. Dick Schultz, secretary of the chapter, said that the chapter regretted that they had not put my talk on tape. He suggested I think about writing a book; that it would not only be entertaining, but a source of interest to the many young people of today who are learning to fly fish or hunt. He asked me to think about it, and he offered to help out. After some deliberation, I told him I would go ahead with it. I realized the amount of work involved, and that it would be a time consuming job. I have since found that to be very true.

As I said, I have been a sportsman for almost seventy years but I have done other things as well. I have raised Christmas trees and race horses and owned a lodge in Canada. While doing those things, I hunted grizzly bears in British Columbia, moose in Ontario, and deer and antelope in the Rocky Mountains of Wyoming. I have fished for salmon in New Brunswick, and for trout and steelhead in all the major streams of Michigan.

I do some painting, mostly water colors of fishing scenes that I take a fancy to when I'm on the stream. I sketch it out in the rough and then try to remember it in my mind. Surprisingly, I have been able to sell some of those paintings to different outdoor magazines. I have also done some wooden decoy duck carvings. But, never in my wildest dreams, did I ever consider writing a book.

That's what this book is about. All the things I have done, and some of the adventures I have had, some funny and some not so funny. I think of all the things I have done, I love fly fishing for trout best of all. It's a magical world for me, and I've never found anything that I enjoyed as much. To me, fishing on a stream for trout is like going to church. I always spend more time sitting and looking than I do actually fishing, and I get a great delight in the beauty of the stream and the woods and water and the animals that I meet. I am a trout fisherman because it gives me great delight to be able to tie a fly, and then go out on a stream and catch a trout with it.

I can have all kinds of problems and be wound up inside, and go out on a trout stream and sit on a log and just watch the stream for a half hour. Then I feel completely relaxed. I don't know how to explain the peacefulness that a running stream in front of me seems to give.

I have always liked fishing with a friend. I had lots of them as you will see in my stories and I have outlived them all. I like to get away to the quiet part of the river by myself and study it, sit and watch, and maybe count the number of times that a particular trout will rise. I love to see and hear the birds, and to watch the deer come to the edge of the water and drink. It is such a beautiful sight that I cannot begin to explain it.

I would like to dedicate this book to the wonderful friends I have had, and who have gone downstream out of sight around the bend of the river. I want them to know that they are still remembered—that there's never a time on the stream now when I am fishing that I don't feel that someone is with me—one of my friends from the past.

I truly believe in immortality and I know there will be trout streams and woods and waters and freshness after I tie my final fly on this earth. I know I will meet all these old friends again, and we will have a great time together. That is my prayer.

John Knowles
December 1992

A Special Tribute
To Mort Neff

This is a special tribute to Mort Neff. In the years he spent on the TV program "Michigan Outdoors," it was a wonderful time to be with this special guy.

I met with him several times in the late forties when he was running his show at top speed. He would call me and ask me to bring my dog along on different pheasant hunts he wanted to photograph for his outdoor show. I spent quite a bit of time with Mort and I got to know him as a friend. I always found him a dedicated, honest human being in every sense of the word.

Two years ago, we at Trout Unlimited had Mort as a guest speaker at our annual meeting. It was a joy for me to meet with him again that night, and to have him sit at our table. I had a friend along by the name of Dan Schultz. Dan was a collector of wildlife art, and he bought several pieces of art that night. Mort and I talked about old times and laughed. Then Mort autographed Dan's pictures at my request, and Dan was really pleased that Mort would do that. That was the kind of a man Mort Neff was—always willing to do anything you asked him as a friend.

After Mort died last year, I felt a real sense of personal loss. He was not only a true friend, but a man who had dedicated his life to the sportsmen of Michigan and had done so much for hunting and fishing in the state. I have some pictures of Mort that we took that night. These photos let Mort know that we haven't forgotten him—that we still revere his efforts to improve hunting and fishing in Michigan, and to thank him for all the good that he did.

John Knowles, Mort Neff, and Dan Schultz

Acknowledgements

No book ever comes to life through the efforts of the author alone. I would like to gratefully acknowledge the help and advice of the following people who have given their time to review and critique my manuscript.

Dr. Larry Van Egeren
Maureen MacLaughlin Morris
Hans R. Lange
Ron Damon
Dan Schultz
The Lansing Writers Group
Judith Birns
Bob Crawford
Carol Edwards
Marne Figenshau
Gail Light
Ray Miller
Bob Schneider
Rich Schultz

Acknowledgements

In addition, I would like to say that this book never would have been written without the help of Dick Schultz who continually encouraged me and spent much of his time helping me put it together. I cannot express my thanks enough for his help.

A Fisherman's Poem

I was all out of sorts so I said to myself,
I'll go fishing today and put all my troubles up on the shelf.
I'll hike to the stream and maybe I'll get some and maybe I
    won't.
But it won't matter much if I do or I don't.
For I'll look at the water and look at the trees,
And soak in the sunshine, and soak up some breeze.

I was all out of step and confused,
My mind was a hodgepodge of stuff;
I had the notion I was falling behind,
And the way I had chosen was going too rough.
I was dealing in dollars and dealing in trade;
And counting my worth by the profits I made.
I'd almost forgotten that the long years might hold,
Some treasures not reckoned in silver and gold.

A Fisherman's Poem

So I went out alone on a beautiful day,
Just to fish and to rest;
And the wind blew a lot of my troubles away
As I later confessed.
And, the Lord came and whispered,
"John, life's more than the sharpening of scissors
Or running a store. You don't need money to live as a friend;
To share in the numerous pleasures I send."

So I stretched out my soul and looked at the trees,
At the clouds drifting by.
I soaked up the sunshine, I soaked up the breeze;
I let my thoughts lie in the beauty of nature,
And birds with their songs.
I measured life's blessings against all of its wrongs.
Set myself straight on things great and small;
And found most of my cares didn't matter at all.

My Early Days In Florida

Although I love cold water fishing in the rivers and streams of northern Michigan, I really learned to fish in the salt water of the Atlantic Ocean. I grew up in Miami in the 1920's and spent my early youth fishing along the Florida Keys like Key Largo and Key West and their many floating islands. The ocean holds a wide variety of fish that are fun to catch.

Several of my friends and I would get together for a weekend, pack a lunch and take off on a fishing excursion with my friend's boat. We did so much fishing that we almost wore the boat out.

We spent a lot of time fishing over shipwrecks in those keys, and we could see boat wreckage clearly in the water below. We didn't know then that in the 1500's, Spanish treasure fleets sailed west from Havana to the Florida Keys in order to follow the Bahama current north along the Florida coast. They sailed through the very waters we were fishing north to St.

Augustine, and then turned east to cross the ocean to Spain. Along the way, they met with tropical storms, English buccaneers and pirates. Many of those Spanish sailors left their bones with their cargoes of gold in the shallow bays and inlets of the Florida Keys. We never realized we were fishing over a fortune in gold, and we never thought of going down to investigate those wrecks. Who knows, we might have found millions, and I often wonder in what direction my life would have went if that had happened. I'll never know.

I remember an old man on one of those islands. He lived in an old tar paper shack that was ready to fall down. It kept him out of the weather and no more but that was enough for him. He lived all alone and he always welcomed us when we came by. He would offer us coffee and give us bait, and in return we would bring him a case of beer, which he really appreciated. One day I asked him, "How on earth do you manage to live on this island? There's nothing here that can provide you with anything to live on."

He grinned at me over his bottle of beer, walked over to a corner of this dirty old shack, and pointed at something covered up by a pile of empty burlap sacks. "I got all I need under there," he said. He lifted up some of those empty sacks and I could see a stack of bricks. I am sure now that this old man had found one of those Spanish wrecks and recovered the gold. I don't know how many gold bricks he had there but I recall them vividly, and I guess there must have been twenty or twenty-five of them. He said, "Whenever I need money, I just take my boat and one of these things and go into Key West to cash it in for whatever I can get for it." It is one of the oddities of an age gone by that an old man we barely knew would trust us with the secret of his cache of gold.

So maybe we should have been fishing for gold instead of

Atlantic flounders. But we were only eighteen year old kids, and had no way of knowing about wrecked Spanish treasure ships in Florida waters. We were always short of money back then, and in those days they were just starting to drain parts of the Everglades to make room for more people. There was a road that ran from Miami and Coral Gables to Homestead on which we could make money.

It was a single dirt road through the Everglades and there was water up to your neck on both sides. I had a Whippet roadster with a rumble seat. Two or three us, mostly kids from my high school football team, drove that road at night looking for alligators. The alligators would be by the roadside or crossing the road. If we kept a sharp lookout in the moonlight, we could sneak up on them. We would stop the car and get out in the dark with a rope and try to loop it around the alligator's nose. If we succeeded, we had to work fast and loop the other end around his tail, and draw the rope up quickly so that the alligator was helpless. Otherwise, he would thrash around with that powerful tail and God help us if we got hit by it. We would throw him in the rumble seat and go on to catch two or three more. Some of those gators were so big that we had a devil of a time getting them in the back of that little Whippet roadster.

Then we would head off to a Seminole Indian village in Hialeah where a Seminole Indian chief we called "Tommy Tommy" lived. I remember him vividly because of his missing ear. He told us that he had had some trouble with his tribe, and as punishment they cut one of his ears off, right at his head. Anyway, Tommy Tommy would give us four dollars for those alligators, and we depended on that money for the rest of the week to buy Cokes and treat our girlfriends.

$4.50 alligators we caught

Those were lean days for some of us in that part of Florida. But I soon found a way to remedy that situation. I guess if my devout Methodist mother had ever found out what I was up to, she would have disowned me on the spot.

Miami wasn't suffering lean times for everybody in the early 1920's. It was in the middle of a real estate boom. The automobile, the railroad, and the airplane were all becoming part of the fabric of Florida life. People were more mobile and were coming to Florida by the thousands. Then the real estate boom collapsed, and in 1926, a hurricane struck the Florida east coast killing over three hundred and ninety people. The hurricane put an end to the selling of real estate in Florida. With the boom times over and the iron hand of prohibition on the country, most people in Florida did what they had to in order to survive. I looked for something that would help me get through college and I found it.

At the end of Flagler Street on Biscayne Bay was a couple of old biplanes parked in the water. The guy who owned them had a sign up, "Fly around Biscayne Bay in an airplane for a dollar." I would stop down there out of curiosity and I got to know him real well. I was interested in airplanes and I helped him work on the motors and put patches on the wings and the canvas fuselage. For all the work I did for him he taught me how to fly. Now in those days, you didn't need a license to fly, and there was no Federal Aviation Commission that controlled it. You just learned to fly by the seat of your pants. He would take me out for half an hour. We would taxi out on to Biscayne Bay and he would turn the controls over to me. One day, I went down there for a lesson and he said, "Kid, go ahead and take it up yourself." All I had to pay for was the gasoline. The plane was called an "OX-Five." There was a radiator right in front of my face. But, I took it up by myself, and flew it, and I became a real competent flyer. That was when the fun began.

One day I said to him, "Bert. That sign on the road intrigues me. It says you'll take people around Biscayne Bay for a dollar. But I don't think I've seen two customers in the whole time I've been here. How the heck do you pay your rent and your upkeep with no money coming in?"

Bert smiled at me and said, "I wondered how long it would take for you to ask that question. Come back tonight about five o'clock and I'll show you."

5

I went back that night at five like he said. He put me in the back seat of one of his airplanes and we flew out over the ocean. We flew to an island called Bimini in the Bahamas. He taxied up to an old ramshackle dock and boat house, and a couple of hard looking guys came out with guns strapped to their waist. I thought, "O lord, what's gonna happen now." They tied the airplane up to the dock and started throwing gunny sacks full of whiskey packed in straw into the back seat on my lap. They got in as many as they could, I think it was seven or eight, and Bert told them to shove off and we turned around and flew back to Miami. He found a spot south of Miami and flew along the coastline at a low altitude just above the water. A parked car flashed its lights a couple of times. Bert taxied in and pulled the pontoons up on the sand. A couple of guys came running out of the car and grabbed the whiskey. We got out and pushed the aircraft off, turned it around, and went back to his base on Flagler Street in Miami.

After we got back, Bert said to me, "I have two aircraft here that are usable. Once a week you can make a trip with me. You can follow me over to Bimini and follow me back, and land where I land and I'll give you fifty bucks a trip."

I was happy to do it. As I said, my mother was a devout Methodist and wanted me to be a minister. If she knew what I was doing, it would have hurt her very badly. But to the day she died, she never knew that at one time in my life I was a rum runner. Fifty dollars in those days seemed like fifty thousand dollars to me, especially to a kid going to the University of Miami. I loaned other kids money. Ten dollars, twenty dollars—I had a collection of notes from all my friends. They would come to me and borrow money because they wanted to take a girl out that night and they didn't have money enough to finance the trip. I think back on those times and I regret being involved with that whole business. Still in fairness to me, the average person regarded prohibition as a joke and bootleg whiskey was a very common thing. It was easy money but for me, most of all, it meant I could fly and that was what I really loved to do.

2

My Early Days Of Fly Fishing

My love for fly fishing began in 1928 when I worked for the *Detroit Free Press* as a police reporter. Charlie Merrell worked in the advertising department of the *Free Press*. He was an avid fly fisherman and a bachelor who lived alone, except for two collie dogs that he loved dearly and took everywhere with him. Charlie and I got to talking about fishing one day, and he invited me to attend his fly fishing club that met every week at the Grand River Sea Food Restaurant.

I went and met a great bunch of guys: Doc Kimble, Tom Harris, Ray Bergman, Holly Blossom, Ken Cooper, Ward Smith, and Earl Parcells. They initiated me into the mysteries of fly fishing, and I became part of a fraternity in Detroit whose members would have an impact on the future of fly fishing not only in Michigan, but throughout the United States and Canada. With them I had many great adventures and a lot of fun. They were pranksters and fun loving guys but deep down they loved the sport of fly fishing and were devoted to it.

I can remember being invited to Charlie Merrell's cabin on the Au Sable River just outside of Roscommon in northern Michigan. It was there I learned to fly fish. Charlie called his cabin "Nippawasee" which is Indian for "Camp On The River." He bought it from a guy across and down the road a bit named Frank Galnick. Frank's father and mother came into the area before the turn of the century with an ox team and a wagon load of all their household goods, and set up living right in the wilderness on the Au Sable River. They built a bridge across the river, and when Charlie came along and saw that bridge and the outstanding view down river of the Au Sable, he fell in love with it. Frank's mother was still alive when Charlie bought the property from them.

Tom Harris

Ken Cooper was the manager of the Hudson Department Store's sporting goods department. We often met at Hudson's just to buy some of the excellent flies that Ken tied. He was a gifted fly tier. His best fly was a large white streamer that really produced at night. I still have some of those flies in my fly box after all these years.

Tom Harris introduced me to night fishing. He was a canny little guy and a marvelous night fisherman. He would be at the cabin almost every weekend. He would loll around in the hammock and have fun during the day. Promptly, every night at eight o'clock, he would head out for the river, and we wouldn't see him again until the wee hours of the morning. Then he would come in about three or four A.M., wake everybody up and dump a creel full of gorgeous brown trout in the sink. He never revealed any of his secret spots.

Another fisherman who came up to Charlie's cabin was Ray Bergman. Ray was the first fly fisherman I ever saw to get down on his knees in his waders, and creep up to a rising trout to get into casting position. He released almost all his fish. He was one of the forerunners of the way to carefully take a hook out of a fish's mouth and release the fish without injuring it. His way of doing it was to push the hook through and cut the barb off. I watched him do it many times on the stream. He carried a pair of pliers in his fishing vest for that purpose. Ray was a heckuva of a fly tier too. One weekend, he brought up a new fly he designed himself. He called it a blue winged Adams, and he tied it on number twelve and fourteen size hooks. He tied a whole bunch of that particular fly for us to use that weekend. We went out on the Au Sable River and it was one of those magic days for fly fishing. The trout just went mad over that pattern. It was the most fantastic fly; everybody was enthusiastic about it.

But of all the guys in the club, the one I remember best is Doc Kimble. He took me under his wing and taught me everything he knew about fly fishing. One day, at our meeting in downtown Detroit, he brought in a hand-made, hand-forged fly tying vise and gave it to me. He had it made on a stand, and I have had the vise since 1928. It is still an excellent crafts-man's tool and is as workable as it was the day Doc gave it to me.

Later on, I met two wonderful fly fishermen who were to have a big impact on fly fishing. One was Lyle Dickerson and the other was Paul Young. In fact, the Trout Unlimited chapter in Detroit is named after Paul Young. They both made fishing rods and there was a terrific rivalry between them. The fisher-men who owned a Lyle Dickerson rod were on one side, and those who owned a Paul Young rod were on the other. They both made wonderful rods, but in my opinion Lyle Dickerson's were the best. There were none that were any better.

Lyle built his rods in a little machine shop he had on Bewick Avenue just off Jefferson on Detroit's east side. It was in a garage behind his house and he made his own machinery, his own mills and everything he needed to build a fly rod. Paul Young's shop was on the other side of Detroit on Grand River Avenue. I bought some of Paul's rods but what I remember best about Paul Young was a fly he tied. He called it the "Adams Straw Man." It was made out of deer hair in the shape of a bug of some kind. Everybody went nuts over that fly and it did a lot to help Paul's shop. His wife tied the flies for him and she was a very good fisherman as well. I met them both several times, years later in Canada, up on the Miramichi River, fly fishing for the fresh run salmon in the summer. But, as I said, my choice for a fly rod was one of Lyle Dickerson's. I would go over to Bewick Avenue to see him and he would have a couple of fly rods made up and want to try them out. We would go out some place together and fish and compare the rods and the line weights.

Lyle Dickerson was a perfectionist in everything. His rods were delicate, lightweight magic wands. During the time I was in Detroit, I must have bought forty or fifty from him. Dick made a two ounce, seven foot rod that I still have and that's dated 1934. It's never been used or had a line on it. I was offered an awful lot of money for it. I bought Dick's rods for about $75.00 or $80.00 apiece and I wish I had a lot more of them.

I called Dick one day from my office. He had moved up to Belaire and retired in a cabin or a cottage or whatever. I finally got him on the phone, and I said, "This is John Knowles. I want to pick up another two or three of your rods. That is, if you have any on hand?"

Dick just laughed at me. He said, "John. You know as well as I do that my rods are museum pieces and there isn't a one to be had anywhere."

I had to agree with him. They were certainly museum pieces and I wish I had more of them. They felt like they were alive when you cast with one of them.

As the years went by, I became more proficient with a fly rod, and eventually graduated to tying my own flies. And I actually caught fish with them.

Then one day, I discovered a river called the South Branch of the Au Sable in the northern part of the lower peninsula of Michigan. There was a club located there called the Ox Bow Club, and I was invited by one its members, Francis Phelps, to visit with them. He introduced me to the people at the club, and then took me over next door, and I met another avid fisherman named George Mason.

George Mason is the sportsman who donated all that beautiful land known at the "Mason Tract" on the South Branch of the Au Sable to the people of Michigan. He was president of Kelvinator and had his own aircraft. He built his own landing field up there. He would fly up there every weekend just to fish. He was an ardent, dedicated, devoted trout fisherman and one of the nicest guys I have ever met. He was a great big guy, and I would see him going down the river past me, and wonder how he ever got in and out his boat because he was so big. He was also a generous, happy, loving man. Many times he invited us over to dinner at his house next door to the Ox Bow Club. He would bring in a big pitcher of martinis after the day's fishing was over and sit around and talk with us. I gave him a lot of flies that I had tied. I don't know whether he ever used them but he always seemed to appreciate them. We became pretty good friends. George was the original founder of Trout Unlimited. He was really hepped up about saving cold water fisheries. This was about the time that he was trying to get the show on the road for Trout Unlimited.

I bought my first membership for Trout Unlimited from a fellow by the name of Vic Beresford. I met him one day at a store in East Lansing, and he waved this book of membership forms to Trout Unlimited under my nose. Of course, he didn't need to sell me on the value of saving cold water fisheries. I enrolled right on the spot and I have been a member ever since, almost from the start of the founding of Trout Unlimited.

During the early years of our fishing club, we would meet at different homes and spend the evening tying flies. It was at one of these meetings that I met Phil Armstrong. He was always playing around with fly lines. I remember him splicing different sections of lines together. He had an idea about a weight forward line, and he would splice different sections of line

13

together and take it out and try it. We would all give it a test, then he would cut it up and splice it together again. I still have one of the original lines that Phil Armstrong spliced together to make a weight forward line.

One day, he came to our meeting at the Grand River Sea Food Restaurant. He had a fly line with him that he thought was just about perfect. We passed it around and looked at it and gave it a lot of thought. It just happened that we had a couple of guests that day from fishing tackle manufacturers. They looked at that line and talked to Phil for a long time about it. It didn't surprise me too much when about six months later, a bug taper line was put on the market for sale by one of those companies. So it was Phil Armstrong who developed the first bug taper or weight forward line that was ever offered to the public.

There were several other things that our club members contributed to fly fishing. Fred Glass (Fred joined our club later) and myself, I believe, really started the trend of light tackle fishing for salmon in Canada on the Miramichi River. We were the first to take a pair of pliers and punch down the barbs on our salmon fly hooks so that we could more easily remove them from the jaws of the salmon. Incidentally, today the law on the Miramichi River requires that barbless hooks be used for salmon fishing. Ken Cooper was the first fly tier to tie a fly for an upside down streamer. He took a hook and bent it with a pair of pliers and we were the first to use it. It worked well because the hook was upside down and we didn't hook up with under-water debris nearly so much.

They were great individuals, always innovating, because they loved fly fishing so much. Their ideas have passed on to a new generation and are now part of the world of fly fishing today. It was a privilege and a pleasure for me to have shared those exhilarating times with them and to have been a part of so many new ideas.

3

Night Fishing For Trout

There is something about night fishing that has always made it my favorite kind of fly fishing. I guess maybe it's the quietness and the mystery, and the unexpected things that you run into while night fishing on the river when the big browns prowl for food. You never know what's going to happen.

I always use a wet fly at night. I fish across and down the river with a fast retrieve on the line. I use the riffling hitch on all my flies and make it a point to rub the fly on the sides of the first fish I catch. I am sure this helps because it gives a scent to the fly, and I have caught some monstrous browns at night; bigger than anything I ever hooked during the day. That too has made me a devoted night fisherman. It's difficult to fish a stream in the darkness and to gauge just how far to throw the fly. I usually take time during the day to run the stretch of stream I am going to fish that night and locate the deep holes and the possible places where fish will lie. It's intriguing because the river seems altogether different at night then during the day. I have an awful time tying flies on at night. You need one of those little flashlights that attach to your vest, and you have to keep it from shining in the water, or you will put the fish down. It takes me a long time to change a fly at night, and the only time I do is when I break off on a fish. I use a special fly that an old fly tier in Maine gave me and stick to it exclusively. It's a size six or eight streamer and has been wonderfully productive for me all through the years.

Once I took a friend night fishing and he was scared to death of it. He was a good fisherman but he just didn't like walking that stream at night. The water is black and dark and it's like wading through a sea of ink. You have to feel with your feet for every rock and boulder, and you absolutely must know ahead of time where all the deep holes are.

I suggested to him that I go first and he follow behind a couple of fly line lengths, so I could guide him around all the deep holes. There was a light moon out and the surface of the water was covered with shadows from the trees. I wasn't catching anything but I could hear him behind me, and I could see his silhouette through the darkness. He was making hook up after hook up. Every time he hooked up, he would break off, and he would yell for me to come help him. By the time I got back there, the fish would be gone. We fished the whole length of that stream and got out just where I planned to leave the water and he never landed even one fish.

It was two o'clock in the morning and I was glad to quit. I was upset by the fact that I hadn't caught a thing, and that he had hooked into all kinds of fish. I don't know whether I disturbed them or whether they avoided me and just ran into his flies. I have never been able to figure that night out.

I had another friend that liked to night fish. His name was

Ed Bligh, and he owned a bunch of apartments in Detroit. One night we went up to the South Branch of the Au Sable and waited until about eight o'clock to start fishing. Ed was about fifty yards behind me and was following my pattern down the river, watching where I stepped. I could just make out his silhouette back in the darkness against the night sky.

We came to a part of the river where the current was fairly strong and channeled through a deep undercut along the river bank. I knew the water was over my head so I moved over to the opposite bank. Ed must have been intent on a fish and missed seeing me in the darkness, because all of sudden, I heard a loud yell and a splash and I knew Ed had taken a dive. I looked back and thought I could see him thrashing around, trying to hold his rod up out of the water and yelling like a banshee for help. Luckily, the current grabbed him and tumbled him downstream right towards me. He was kicking and sputtering and I could guess that his waders were filling with water which would drag him under for good. I put my rod in my left hand and reached out with my right. I grabbed him by the neck and his wader suspenders and tugged him to shore. I pulled his waders and his pants off, and he stood there in his underwear, shivering and shaking in the cold night air. I got a fire going while he stripped to the buff, and you would have thought he would have huddled next to that fire to keep warm. Instead, he began dancing up and down and shouting at me, "My pants, my pants, give me my pants."

"What?" I said. I didn't know what he was talking about. "Your pants are all soaking wet, Ed. You don't want to put those on till they're dry. Nobody's going to see you here naked."

"I know. I know." He shouted. "Just give me those damn pants."

18

I thought to myself, "That's a funny thing to do. To shout at a guy who had just saved his life." Well, I found them in the darkness and gave them to him. He reached in his back pocket and pulled out his wallet.

"Damn," he muttered. He opened up the wallet and pulled out one of the biggest wads of money I had ever seen. There must have been three or four thousand dollars in fifty and one hundred dollar bills. He wrung the river water out of them and then spread them out to dry around the fire. I tried not to laugh too loud. There Ed stood stark naked in the firelight, wringing out fifty and one hundred dollar bills and laying them out to dry. After his money and his clothes dried out, he put the money back in his wallet, put his clothes on, and we went fishing again and caught some real nice fish.

When we got back home in Detroit, Ed went around telling everybody how wonderful it was of John to have saved him from drowning. *Now,* if the truth must come out, the real reason I grabbed Ed by the neck and hauled him out of the river was that with all the commotion he was making, I was afraid he would put down all the trout in the pool I was fishing. Besides, as I think about it now, if he had lost that wallet in the river, we would have spent the entire night fishing for the billfold instead of fish.

Night fishing is always a wonderful time of solitude and quiet for me. You hear the fish feeding and all kinds of other night noise behind you in the woods. In the back of your mind you wonder if it's a bear but usually it's a deer or a coon or some other animal. But surprises can and do happen and you never know what you're going to run into next. I love it.

I have spent a lot of time night fishing on the South Branch of the Au Sable, especially in the 1930's. I remember a place where I camped back then that is now called Canoe Harbor. It's

19

been expanded into a great big place where you can pitch a tent and stay. But in the 1930's, it was just a single track dirt road through the pines back to the river. We would park there and there was never anyone else around; you never saw another car. We could walk down to the river along a deer trail lined with tall ferns. They were huge and covered over the top of the trail, and you had to watch carefully where you were going. I can still remember the wonderful odor of those ferns. At about seven thirty at night, we would walk down the path through that valley of ferns and sit on the bank of the river. We would just sit there and listen to the sounds of the evening all around us. Then, a little after eight, the whippoorwills would start to call. We knew then it was time to go fishing. It was like they were giving us a signal. If we went in the water before the whippoorwills started calling, we would get skunked.

The South Branch will always be my favorite stream. There were many deep holes in it, and I can remember every one. I got to know where the big trout were likely to be on the river. Fishing at night on the South Branch was a special experience when one of those tremendous mayfly hatches came on. The big browns turned into hogs on a night like that. But we were never anxious to keep fish, even in those days. We would catch eighteen to twenty inch browns, and we returned almost everything we caught. I never could bear to kill them. So I would put them back in the water carefully. I didn't know then that you had to push them back and forth in the water to aerate them and get the gas out of their stomach. I just turned them loose and they certainly took off in a hurry.

I can remember fishing the big Michigan mayfly hatch on the main branch of the Au Sable down below Mio many years ago. We would go downstream, find a spot, park our car, take a place on the bank in front of the river and sit down and wait.

There would be fishermen all along the stream for miles doing the same thing, just sitting with their rods, smoking, waiting and watching. You would sit there sometimes for hours and finally after dark, you'd hear a faint cry from some fisherman way upstream, "Here they come." And in a few minutes, the next guy up the river would shout, "Here they come." The shout would follow right down to where we were sitting. The next thing we knew, almost from nowhere, a great cloud of those big mayflies would appear.

Until then there wouldn't be a sign of any trout in front of you. But when those flies came down on the water, the whole river would be alive with feeding trout. Immense big browns that you would never see earlier in the summer. The flies would be so numerous and so thick that when you got up to fish, they covered you like a wet, heavy snow. They would get in your eyes and ears, and down the back of your neck, and in your mouth. We would fish with heavy leaders. We would pick out a rising trout in the water and cover him with a fly just as quick as we could. When we hooked up, we would get that trout out of the water just as fast as we could so we could get our fly back to another fish. Sometimes you could catch two or three trout before the flies rolled on down past you and the fish stopped feeding. I have had as long as half an hour to almost three quarters of an hour of really good fishing on some of those hatches. Fisherman came from all over the United States to fish that mayfly hatch. It was that exciting.

There was another place on the South Branch of the Au Sable where we fished a caddis hatch. We called it the High Banks. It was a big deep bend with sweepers and overhangs. It was a tough place to fish; in fact, it was almost impossible to fish it except during the caddis hatch. That was the only time that the fish would come out from behind all that broccoli and you had a chance to hook them before they swam back under the logs. I can remember many times catching eighteen-, twenty-, twenty-two-inch browns in there—some even bigger. We never failed to catch fish when we went to the High Banks if we were lucky enough to find a caddis hatch. Sometimes we would hit a hatch and sometimes we wouldn't. We could go there and spend the entire night and not have a single fish to show for it. But when we hit the bonanza at the right time, we could really bring in the browns.

In those early days, we did a lot of night fishing on the Au Sable River below the Consumer's Power dam at Mio, Michigan. It was a strong river to fish and I had many hair-raising experiences on it. We would be out in the middle of the river fishing at night and Consumers would open the gates and that water would come down the river in a rush. If we were in the middle of the river fishing, it could strand us there and we would have one helluva time getting back to shore trying to buck that current. It was a dangerous part of the river to fish and we had to keep our eyes open in case Consumer's decided to open the dam. But generally speaking, the river itself from the dam to about two miles down below, was a wonderful place to fish and to catch big brown trout, especially at night. It was really wild up there in those days. Many times we saw bear down along the river. A couple of times they chased us out of the river.

People would float that river in boats and canoes and I have seen some real serious accidents. One particular time, a couple of guys came in a canoe from the dam down to where we were fishing when Consumers decided to lower the water behind the dam. The rush of water and the current got a hold of them and upset the canoe. One guy made a wild leap for a branch of one of the overhanging trees. He hung there for the longest time, his feet dangling in the water. He must have hung there for about five minutes before he finally let go and dropped into the water. Fortunately, he was able to swim and got to shore all right. But both guys lost all their equipment, their fly rods, and even the canoe. I'll venture to say that particular stretch below Mio has a lot of good tackle in it that no one has ever found.

It's a strange thing, but of all the time I fished up by Mio, I never fished above the dam, and I know that the main stream of the Au Sable up above the dam was full of fish. I knew all the spots on that river a mile or so below the dam, and I knew where it was deep and wadeable. I fished at night and we had to be careful, even when we knew the river as well as we did. We studied the river by day and would find out where the deep pockets were and try to fish them at night. We were usually quite successful.

When I night fish there is absolutely nothing in the woods that I fear. I love the night sounds and the quietness and the excitement of hearing the different animals in the woods along a river at night. But bats are something else. How many times I have had bats diving and swirling around my head when I am fishing at night—and bats upset me a great deal! They especially bother me when one of them takes my fly on a back cast, and I suddenly find that my forward cast has stopped in the air with a bat squealing and hollering and flopping on the end of my line. I would like someone to tell me how to take one of these critters off my line and take the fly out of its mouth. I hate the sight of them. They bite like hell and cause a lot of commotion that can put the fish down.

I remember a pool on a logging stream that was just filled with old logs from the lumbering days. It was a wonderful place to fish; I would go there in the evening just before dark. But that pool was infested with bats. There wasn't a night I went there that I didn't have bats around me; it got so I was afraid to go there. Those things would fly around and hit my hat and run into my neck. They would do just about everything to drive me off that river. I can't count how many times I have hooked one in the air—how they could catch that fly in the air was beyond me, but they could do it. I finally took a pair of leather gloves and a can of yellow spray paint along. I would hold a bat with my leather gloves, remove the hook, and put a touch of paint on it. Do you know I caught one of those damn things three times in a row! Just the same, night fishing will always be my favorite pastime, bats and all. It is a magical time to be fishing.

4

Tales Of The Biffy

As I said before, that old gang in Detroit that taught me to fly fish was filled with great innovators. They had their fun side too. They were great pranksters and really enjoyed catching someone in a practical joke. I recall a black bear hide that Charlie Merrell owned—it still had the head attached to it. When somebody new came up to the cabin and went out to the biffy, one of us would take the bearskin, throw it over our shoulders and follow him out there. When the new guest had settled himself in and was peacefully contemplating the serenity of the woods, the guy with the bearskin would get down on his knees by the biffy and growl and in general make a lot of noise. The new guy would poke his head out the door to see what was going on. When he caught sight of that bear, his duty to nature ended right then. He would come tearing out of that biffy, trying to pull up his pants and run at the same time. The rest of us would be waiting outside the cabin, smirking as he came running up. Sometimes the guy would be so embarrassed that he would sneak off into the woods to do his duty rather than let anybody know he was going to the biffy.

Tom Harris, Charlie Merrill, and Frank Galnick

Once Doc Kimble spent a whole weekend that he could have been fishing wiring the seat of that outhouse with a speaker. He put the speaker under the seat and then connected it to a microphone in the cabin. Then we would wait patiently for a new guest to go out to the biffy. When we knew he was settled in, Doc would speak into the microphone and say very quietly, "Hi up there. We're painting down here. Would you mind moving over just a little bit?" Often one of the guys

26

brought his wife up for the weekend in order to prove where he was spending all his time. Every time we all looked forward to when that girl would go back to the biffy, and Doc Kimble would talk into that microphone. That was his pet job and he delighted in it. He would get to laughing so hard, he would almost choke. Those women would come charging out of that backhouse, trying to arrange their dresses, wondering what the heck was going on.

Once, when Doc Kimble was wiring the speaker under the outhouse seat, Charlie Merrell stood outside watching him and making wisecracks. Finally, Doc got tired of listening to him and said, "Charlie, you'll have to help. I just dropped my screwdriver down the hole and you're smaller than me. I'll hold you by the legs and you can go down the hole and retrieve it."

Charlie looked at Doc for a long time studying his face. Doc never cracked a smile. Finally, Charlie said, "Doc, you know I never did like that screwdriver. And, I wouldn't trust you any farther than I could throw a bull by the horns. So you can go to hell."

We always had all kinds of fun. They were wonderful guys. They would do anything in the world for you. They would loan you their best fly rod or flies or even their waders if you needed them. Doc Kimble offered me his waders one day when I forgot mine. I laughed when I put those waders on. They were about ten sizes too big for me and they must have had a hundred and fifty patches on them.

We had some other great times too. We tried to give something back to the people in northern Michigan. I can remember the little town of South Branch was without fire equipment back in the thirties. So Fred Glass, who joined our fly fishing fraternity later on, and I went to the City of Detroit and bought an old fire engine, a complete pumper. It had hoses

Town Turns In Its Buckets for a Big Red Fire Engine

SOUTHBRANCH, Mich. (Pop. 100) retired its bucket brigade Saturday and the residents took turns swinging the town's first fire engine (vintage 1920) around the village square.

The town, "just a wide spot in the road in Ogemaw County," according to Paul Schlenker, co-owner of a resort, is thankful to three Detroit deer hunters for modernizing its fire department. Southbranch has converted an ice house into a fire station.

While 50 townspeople were gathered at Schlenker's tavern to discuss the deplorable state of Southbranch's fire fighting fund (total assets $60 from raffle of a rifle), they heard a terrific din.

Roaring through town in a second-hand Detroit fire engine were Fred N. Glass, Jr., 8992 Griggs avenue, co-pilot; John Knowles, 3858 Yorkshire road, Grosse Pointe, pilot, and Karl Koepplinger, 4803 Outer drive west, official "bell ringer and door slammer."

Knowles, who had driven the engine 186 miles from Detroit in sub-freezing weather, said the three hunters had been visiting South Branch for 20 years. They had heard of the plight of the village fire department. They decided to do something about it. For $1 the town could have the engine.

Mrs. Schlenker, whose home burned down a year ago, burst into tears. So did two farmers and several cottage owners who had suffered fire damage in the last few years.

"I'll equip it with a 1,000-gallon tank," shouted Ed Grieves, village president. "I'll convert my ice house," said Schlenker.

Knowles said the engine cost $200. He said the three men had harbored a secret ambition to drive a fire engine, and "this was a chance to do just that and also help out some wonderful people."

and ladders, the complete works for a fire truck. The City of Detroit was going to trade it in for new equipment so we bought it for $200. One of our friends was Karl Koeplinger who owned Koeplinger Bakery. He was another member of our fly fishing club. One weekend, Karl, Fred, and I took this fire engine up to South Branch. It had an open cab and it was wintertime, but we drove it all the way up to South Branch from Detroit, a distance of over 160 miles.

We drove around downtown South Branch with the bells ringing, siren going, and the lights flashing. People came running from all over wondering what the hell was going on. Eventually, we ended up at the town hall where we presented them with this fire engine. Right then and there, they made Karl, Fred, and myself deputy fire chiefs. They were so grateful for the fire engine that they would do almost anything for us. South Branch was a great place to fish and I have many fond memories of the place.

One year during a deer hunting trip, I had flown up to South Branch with a friend in an open cockpit Waco, a two-seater biplane. Wouldn't you know it, even though it was my friend's first deer hunting trip, he bagged himself a deer. Now we had a problem. How were we ever going to get that deer back to Detroit in a two-seater airplane? Something had to give and that something was him. He was the one that shot it and he was the one that wanted to bring that deer back.

The only way we could do it was to set the deer on his lap in the back seat and put the strap around him to hold him and the deer in place. I remember thinking how silly he looked with that deer sitting on his lap in the back seat with his arms wrapped around it, and the deer head with its rack of horns sticking out like it was the passenger. I thought maybe we should put some goggles on the deer just to make it look official. Anyway, it worked quite well and we got back to Detroit without incident. It caused quite a stir at the airport because when we landed all anyone could see was the deer head sticking out of the back seat. It got quite a laugh and for awhile everyone was making jokes about it. From then on my fly-in deer hunting trips were made with the idea of how we were going to transport the deer we had shot.

5

Rainbows On The Sturgeon And Other Fishing Stories

In my scrapbook of fishing trips, I have a folded paper outline of a rainbow trout that I caught on the Sturgeon River near the town of Indian River in northern lower Michigan. On this outline I have written, "Rainbow trout. Caught on the Sturgeon River, August 21st, 1937, by John Knowles. Length 19¾ inches, weight 3 pounds. Time of day caught: 9:30 A.M. Water clear. Fly used: Deer hair streamer, wet." That was nearly sixty years ago, and I can still recall taking that fish.

I really discovered the Sturgeon River early in the 1930's when my wife Marge and I went to the Indian River for our two-week vacation. I had heard about the fishing and the sturgeon in Burt Lake and I was able to convince her that it was a grand place to spend a vacation. My wife doesn't like to fish. In those early days, she just went along to relax and take it easy; she usually stayed at the cabin when I went fishing. The first day I walked down to the mouth of the Sturgeon River where it ran into Burt Lake. I noticed a number of things down there. First of all, there were many boats with fishermen—twenty or thirty boats parked right on the mouth of the river.

There were rainbows trying to get up the river to spawn, but the river had filled in an area at the mouth with sand from runoff. There were only about twelve or fourteen inches of water over the sand. Those poor rainbows wouldn't cross through that stretch of shallow water because they were so visible. Birds were flying above them and people were striking at them with nets. Other fishermen were fishing in the deep part of the lake right on the edge of the runoff. I looked at that mess and started to wonder what could be done about it. The rainbows needed to get up the river to spawn and they were not making it now. Unless they succeeded, any future runs of rainbows up that river would probably be nil.

That night I called a friend, Chuck Reed, who lived in Indian River. We talked about how the runoff at the mouth of the river was stopping the fish from going upstream, and decided to get a bunch of guys together from Indian River and see what could be done about it. It took a couple of days to get the word around but eventually a number of dedicated fishermen who lived near Indian River showed up for a meeting. We all agreed that quick action was needed and we decided to drive spiles in the edge of the river mouth so that they would increase the flow of water, wash the sand out and deepen the entrance to the river. With the river deepened at the mouth, we felt sure the rainbows would be able to make their spawning run upriver. I spent my whole vacation that year working with those people. They were willing workers and were very interested in the conservation part of improving the river, because it meant revenue for many of them. Some of them owned gas stations, restaurants, cabins and what not.

It was hard and heavy work. The spiles were twelve to fifteen feet long and about six inches in diameter, and each one had to be hand driven into the edge of the riverbank. We got the job finished and you wouldn't believe the difference—the river actually washed the sand away and dug a trench right into the lake. As soon as the sand was cleared away, the rainbows took off right upriver. A lot of those boat fishermen raised hell about it. They even tried to prevent us from doing the work, because they had been catching fish as if they were fishing in a fish pond before. When we opened up the mouth of the river, the fish had security in the depth of the water, and they could go upstream without being chased and hampered by all those boats and fishermen. I have an article that was run in the *Free Press* about the work we did. It was a nice piece of conservation on our part and I received many comments about it from people in Detroit and other places. Above all, I got personal satisfaction from doing something worthwhile to improve the fishing in the river.

I fished the river for years after that and caught a lot of nice rainbows there. The one I mentioned at the start of this story was only one of many. I kept those measurements to remind me of the great fishing for rainbows after we improved the river.

The Sturgeon River is well known in Michigan and has been fished pretty heavily through the years. But sometimes my fishing trips have taken me to trout streams that were practically untouched. Such a stream was one I found in the upper peninsula of Michigan north of L'Anse up by the Lake Superior shore. I only fished it once many years ago. As remote as the stream is I know that I could take someone back there and still find it today.

WOODS and WATERS
—By Jack Van Coevering 1939—

WE ARE glad to relate this morning the story of an unselfish piece of conservation work just completed by the sportsmen and business men of Indian River. It so happens that John Knowles, of Detroit, went up there in quest of rainbow trout a week or so ago. He fished the Sturgeon above Indian River, and while he caught a few, the fishing did not compare at all with that of last year.

When he began to check on the matter, he discovered that the Sturgeon River had been dumping a lot of sand into Burt Lake, until finally the mouth was almost closed by a sand bar. The water was not even a foot deep over the bar. John found some 25 boats anchored just beyond the bar, which remained there 24 hours of the day, in order not to lose their choice fishing spots. Anglers sat in the boats and caught rainbows easily as these fish milled about, seeking a channel through which to swim upstream. In addition to the anglers, John found hundreds of gulls flying about, ready to pounce on any trout which should venture on the shallow sand bar.

John figured this was bad business, and talked the matter over with Chub Reed, who operates a string of tourist cabins in Indian River. Reed took the matter to heart, canvassed the rest of the business men and sportsmen in the town, took up a collection for materials, organized a gang of some two dozen men, and called for a construction bee. Soon the boys had the channel deepened. They built wing dams to keep the current flowing, and now the big rainbows are swimming up the Sturgeon without hindrance.

This sort of initiative deserves a hand. The Indian River group believes that the Conservation Department should put in some permanent wing dams with spiles so that the bar will not form again, but they did not wait for State officialdom to move when the need arose. They dug down into their own pockets and furnished their own labor and did the job when it needed doing. That's good sportsmanship and real conservation.

Three of us found that stream—Larry Dreffs, Ralph Link and myself. It was November, 1946, and we were in L'Anse looking for a place to deer hunt. We drove north out of L'Anse about ten or fifteen miles to the end of the road we were on. We got out and surveyed the land and decided that this was the place where we wanted to hunt. We turned the car around and started back to town to find a place to stay. As we drove along, we came upon an elderly gentleman with a pack sack on his back. Because we were so far out from town, I pulled over to the side of the road and called to him, "If you're going into town, would you like a lift?"

He said, "I would love it." He got in the car and we chatted about the weather and how beautiful the country was up that way. Finally, he said, "Well, I'm going into work. But, I guess you boys are up here to go deer hunting. You got a place to stay?"

I said, "No. We're headed into L'Anse right now to find a motel."

He said, "You don't want to stay in a motel in the middle of town when there's so much beautiful country out here." Then, he shouted at the top of his voice, "Stop the car!" It was such a sudden shout and it surprised me so much, I didn't know how to react. Finally, I stopped the car and apologized to him because I thought somehow we had offended him.

He looked the three of us over quite closely, looking directly into the face of each of us in turn. Then he said, "No, I don't want to get out. But, I've got a cabin back there in the bush where you guys can stay. You don't have to go into town."

We didn't know what to make of that, but to humor him we turned the car around and drove back four or five miles to a path off the road. We followed the path a ways till we came to a clearing, and there on the edge of the clearing was a small log cabin sitting at the edge of a beautiful sparkling trout stream. One dreams of settings like that for a cabin. It was almost like magic to find this one. He got out of the car and opened the door and we went inside. The cabin was completely furnished with home made furniture, and the walls were covered with guns and fishing rods. It was the perfect hunting cabin in the woods—secluded and comfortable.

He said, "Here are the keys to the cabin. I'll get a pencil and paper and write down my address in L'Anse. You can drop the key off when you're through. You can stay here as long as you like. Whether it's a week or two weeks, it won't cost you a dime." We didn't know what to say, we were so surprised! Here was a complete stranger giving us the keys to a place that we knew was a very private sanctuary for him.

Finally, I said to him, "How can you do this? We're complete strangers. You don't even know our names. How do you know we won't run off with everything you have in this cabin including the guns and the fishing rods?"

He just shook his head and said, "I study people and I know what kind of people they are when I see them. I know I can trust you. And, I know you'll appreciate what you find here." It was a wonderful thing. We drove him into L'Anse and then turned around and went back to the cabin. We stayed there for ten days. The cabin was fully furnished—it had everything in it a person could want. All his personal things were there—guns and clothing. It was in immaculate shape and we left it that way.

There was a front porch on the cabin that overlooked the trout stream. We would sit out there in the evening and watch the trout rise in the stream. When the moon came up, we could hear wolves running deer way off in the wilderness. They would be miles away from us, but we could still clearly hear them calling to each other. At times it would almost make the hair on the back of our necks stand up.

We had a successful deer hunt and went home reluctantly. The trip didn't cost us very much, but the memory of that cabin in the woods stayed with us. We all promised each other that next spring at the opening of trout season, we would go back and fish that sparkling stream in front of that wonderful cabin.

We went back to L'Anse the next spring just as we promised. We stopped in town to talk to the old man, but the people at the house where he stayed said he had died two months before. That dampened our spirits quite a bit because we had looked forward to talking with him again, and to thank him for his courtesy. We drove out to the cabin, which was deserted. We had a tent and stuck it up on the river in the rear of the cabin and stayed there for three days. We caught more trout in those three days of fishing than I ever caught before in the same length of time. We brought a whole bunch back in an icebox, somewhere around twenty or thirty. The fish must have been any where from eighteen to nineteen inches long. What a ball we had! In my entire life, I have never had such good luck fishing as we had then. But it is the remembrance of the kindness of that old man that I will never forget. The very sad thing is that I have forgotten his name.

I am a very private kind of fisherman. I don't like fishing with crowds on a trout stream. And, if you don't like it, why do it? I would spend hours and days searching out new places to fish, secret spots. I would drive back roads and find a stream or a brook crossing a road. I would take my rod out of its case and would walk miles up and down that stream to find a hidden pool or a beaver dam that I thought other fisherman hadn't yet found. I found a whole bunch of these spots, and when I found them I marked them on a map, and I treasured those finds.

Whenever I found a beaver dam, I felt I had discovered the mother lode. Beaver dams have provided me with fishing that has been out of this world.

It also breaks my heart to find one of those bonanzas, and then go back the following year and find that the Conservation Department has dynamited it early in the spring. I found several beaver dams and secret spots north of Clare, Michigan that you would never believe held trout, and quite a few more north of Rose City and Mio, Michigan. Each one has turned out to be a place where I could depend on good fishing. But time changes these spots and every year when I walk into one I wonder if it is still a secret. Lots of times it isn't.

I found one of these secret spots on a small creek just north of Vanderbilt, Michigan. It was a beaver dam at least fifteen yards across which had created a large pond at its base. I had never seen such a huge structure and I marveled that the beavers could make something like that. The water in the pond was deep, way over my head, and it was full of bright speckled brook trout. The bottom was marl, so there was no way to fish it from shore. One step in that muck and you would sink clear to your neck. The only way to fish it was from the top of the dam itself. After crashing through the brush, I made my way to the top of the dam, got comfortable on it, and started casting for brook trout. Trout started hitting my fly immediately but I found that in order to land the trout, I had to get up and walk to shore where I could reach out and net the fish. It was worth the effort, because I was catching some beautiful fish.

Soon, I had caught several fish and was perched comfortably on top of the dam, my thoughts wandering to far off places, waiting for the next fish to strike. Then I saw something move out of the corner of my eye. What I saw made the hair on the back of my neck stand straight up. I almost dropped my fishing rod in the water. It was the largest, ugliest, coiled snake I had ever seen in Michigan. Now, I have seen a lot of snakes in Michigan, and anybody who tells you there aren't rattlers in Michigan better do a little more research on the subject, because I have seen a lot of them, and this one was the granddaddy of them all.

This snake was coiled with his mouth open. He was hissing and poised to strike. I stood up very slowly and then in one motion turned and jumped off the beaver dam into the pond below with my fly rod in my hand. That pond was so deep that I slipped completely out of sight under the water. I came up sputtering for air, and then had to struggle to get out of that marl bottomed pond. When I finally crawled out, I was covered with muck and mud almost from top to bottom. I would sink so deep in that marl that it almost sucked my waders off. I had to struggle and pull with all my strength to free myself to take each step. After that, whenever I fished that pond behind that beaver dam, (Yes, I went back, the fishing was that good), I always poked around carefully and looked for that snake. I saw several more there after that, but don't know whether any snake I saw later was the same one. The snakes that were there were still huge and they scared the heck out of me. Boy, what a surprise that one gave me!

6

Tales Of The Miramichi

Fred Glass and I had always dreamed of fishing for salmon somewhere in Canada. So back in the early forties, we decided to try it. We met one day at the Wonder Bar in Detroit for lunch and discussed where to go and how to go about it. We had names of some outfitters from sporting magazines and we wrote to several of these people and they answered us. We settled on a guy named Pearlie Calhoun at Boystown, New Brunswick. Pearlie sounded like the best deal we could find. We sent him a deposit and told him we would be there on such and such a date.

We took off from the Windsor airport and landed at Fredericton, New Brunswick where one of the guides from Pearlie's camp picked us up in an old battered car and drove us to Boystown where Pearlie's camp was located. Pearlie Calhoun's staff consisted of his two sons who worked for him, one as a guide and one as a manager of the camp. They were wonderful guys and we got to be real good friends. His camp was a beautiful old lumber camp. It was right on the bank of the Miramichi River with a great view upstream and down. It was a spectacular place to stay. It had a big veranda overlooking the river and we would sit out there at night and drink Moulsens Ale and Crown Royale whiskey and reminisce about the day's fishing.

It was about six o'clock in the evening when we got to the camp and met all the guides, exchanged pleasantries and got acquainted. We had a quite nice time around the dinner table that night talking about fishing and all the places we had been. Eventually, they wanted to see our fishing gear—see what kind of rods and tackle we had brought. When we brought out our fishing rods and showed them to the guides, they looked at each other in surprise. Fred and I had brought two three-ounce fly rods which were considered lightweight fishing rods. We put the rods together and showed them to the guides. They sat there in disbelief and shook their heads. I asked, "Is there something wrong with this gear?"

The guides looked at each other, reluctant to say anything. Finally, one of them said, "You don't expect to catch salmon on those little sticks, do you?"

Fred and I both said, "Well, yes. How big do the salmon up here grow?"

"Hell," one of the guides said. "We get 'em up to twenty-five, thirty pounds. No way you're going to catch and hold them on those little bitty things."

"Well," I said, "We catch fish like that all the time with these rods." The guides sat there and looked at each other, and we knew they were thinking that we were full of it, and that if these rich sports wanted to go out and waste their time fishing that way, well that was up to them. They didn't say any more about it the rest of the night.

The following morning, Fred and I got up and walked down to take a look at the river in front of the camp. It just so happened there was a pool in the river right in front of the camp, and though I didn't know it at the time, there was a nice salmon in that pool. I put my rod together and walked down to the shore in front of the cabin. Believe it or not, I still marvel at it, because I found out later that salmon weren't that easy to catch—I hooked into that salmon and landed it. Beached it right in front of the cabin on top of the bank. The guides were standing there watching closely how I played it. Usually they went downstream and picked the salmon up by the tail rather than net it. To see me bring that salmon in alone without any help really set them off. They had a different look in their eyes when we had breakfast that morning.

Shore lunch on the Miramichi

Fred and I had brought along a fly tying kit and a small vise, even though we had plenty of flies tied up for the trip that we thought would work. Just in case, we bought two or three dozen "summer flies" in Fredericton. We didn't really know which fly would work but we started out with them anyway.

The first morning out, we each had a guide and a canoe. They don't paddle canoes on the Miramichi, they pole them along the edge of the river. It's really something to see those guys stand up in the back of the canoe and push it up the river with a sport sitting in front. They can go long distances that way, and I saw them do it many times.

Anyway, we started fishing and we started catching salmon. We hooked two or three that first morning between us and we had some trouble with them. We broke off one and landed two. They weren't big fish; a little bigger than a grilse but they ran probably eleven or twelve pounds. We were elated with our success on the first morning and so were the guides. The guides were very impressed with our ability to play and handle a fish with those small rods. We had about three hundred yards of backing on each of our reels and we found by letting the fish run way back in the backing, almost to the end of it sometimes, that we had a better chance of playing him out and landing him.

That night in camp, we sat around and tied flies. We had some flies that we thought were better than what they had up there. But, we went ahead and tied a bunch of flies, and the following day we tried them out and one or two of them worked quite well. One was called a Knowles Butterfly. It was named by Fred. The Knowles Butterfly worked extremely well the next day, according to the fishing log that I kept for all my trips. We hooked into a lot of fish. We changed flies to try to adapt and to find which was the best one but we always went back to this Knowles Butterfly. That night we sat around with the guides and we tied about two dozen of these flies. We tied them weighted and unweighted because we wanted to test which fly would work the best. One thing stands out in my memory about that salmon fishing. We were using a fly that was unweighted, and we found that if we put a little bit of copper wire on the hook just before we tied the body and the tinsel on, that it got it down a little further and worked a helluva lot better. We also found that by using the riffling hitch on a fly, it had a better presentation and really drove the salmon nuts.

The second or third day, we caught a whole bunch of salmon. We carefully weighed and measured each salmon and recorded them in the log. Our guides had a habit of going to the local bar in town after each day's fishing and boasting about the salmon their sports caught. Guides came from different camps up and down the river to compare their luck and to talk about their sports and what happened that day. The word got out among these guides at the bar about this Knowles Butterfly. The next day, two or three guys from one of the camps came down after dinner and asked if we could tie some flies for them. It turned into a real fly tying bee for us every night. We would tie flies until we had too much Moulsens Ale to tie any more. We had more people come from up and down the river every day. It was a kind of word-of-mouth advertising. You wouldn't believe how many of those flies we tied and gave away. We never charged these guys anything for them. We were happy to give them something that helped them catch salmon.

There was always ice alongside the river when we went up there in May. Some days it was real cold, and behind the cabin there was quite a bit of snow. When we cleaned fish, we would never open the fish up. We would merely cut the gills out and stash them in the ice. Then the guides would go back in the woods with a chainsaw and make a beautiful pine box for shipping fish—right out of the woods. They packed those fish in fern and ice and moss, and we shipped them through Ottawa marked "Fresh Salmon," and asked that they be re-iced and sent on to our locker in Detroit. When we received those fish in Detroit after we got back, they tasted as if they were caught in the Miramichi River that day.

From my fishing log of May 11, 1940:

> *Morning fishing was poor. Weather clear, sunshine. Morning catch was two grilse around four pounds and eight pounds.*
>
> *Afternoon: Fred and I each caught one good salmon. Fred's twelve pounds and mine eighteen pounds. Wonderful scrappers and a great thrill.*
>
> *Our second day's fishing was voted a huge success. Fred lost two big salmon due to his reel locking up which let the salmon break the line. Afternoon: it rained and we had to quit. It got real cold.*

On our third day, May 13th:

> *Fred had a twelve pound grilse that fought for twenty minutes and jumped fourteen times. Fred left flies in two large salmon in the morning fishing. Broken leaders. And lost two more immense salmon in the afternoon.*
>
> *Fred and I both had a large salmon on at the same time. And, we both lost our salmon simultaneously. Fred's reel backlashed and the salmon broke loose. Mine made a beautiful leap in the air and threw the fly. Fred lost another salmon under a rock. He broke the leader and he had to cross the river to get the line free where*

45

MIRAMICHI RU. Date 5-17-46
Lake or Stream
Located in NEW BRUNSWICK County,
........Miles........ of CANADA
Direction
Weather CLOUDY A.M. Temperature 55°
Time of Day SUNNY. P.M

WE HAD THE BEST LUCK

- ☐ Casting with
- ☐ Trolling with
- ☐ Still fishing with
- ☑ Fly fishing with KNOWLEY BUTTERFLY

Kinds of Fish Caught	No.	Size	Bait
SALMON	JOHN	17. Pos.	VARIOUS FLIES'
GRILSE	FRED	4 Po.	
GRILSE	JOHN		
GRILSE	JOHN		
SALMON	FRED	18 POUNDS -	
GRILSE (6)	FRED	4-5 POUNDS -	

Altogether we caught a total of -11- SALMON fish.
The largest was a SALMON
that was........inches long and weighed 18- lbs.

THOSE IN THE PARTY

Fred
John

it was snagged on a big boulder.

Fourth day, May 14th:

I caught a fourteen pound salmon. The fish put up a great battle, and at one time had all the line and backing out. It was forty-five minutes later and almost a mile down river from where it was hooked before the fish was landed. Joe Case, the guide, waded out almost to his knees to pick up the salmon by the tail.

We shipped our first box of fish home today. A total of fifteen salmon for a hundred and twenty to a hundred and thirty-five pounds. In the afternoon, Fred caught six grilse and kept two. Fred had the thrill of a lifetime with a tremendous fish that he had on for fourteen minutes. The fish threw the fly with a jump six or seven feet out of the water. His guide said it was as large a salmon as he had seen that year. The old bastard's chin is really down tonight. "To hell with fishing," he says.

These are just excerpts from the log. The fishing went on every day just about the same, some days better than others. But we had such a wonderful time up there and so many pleasant memories, we decided to go the next year.

That started the ball rolling, because we made eleven trips up there in all, and we took different people and introduced them to the salmon fishing. As the years went by, the guides got older and knew us better and we had a better time of it. We renewed friendships every year. It was a wonderful experience. I don't know of any better way to end a the report of our first experience in New Brunswick than by looking at the log and the total fish caught.

Our recap read:

Eight days total. Fred caught thirty-five grilse and nine salmon. John caught twenty grilse and ten salmon.

It rained all morning and fishing was poor. John and Joe Case, the guide, saw a big black bear cross the clearing and went back to camp for a gun, but no luck. A neighbor said he saw twelve to fourteen bear there in the same clearing last fall. We hit the jackpot in the afternoon. John took three good salmon and Fred took one. We shipped our second box of fish tonight. There were sixteen salmon and five grilse in the box. It was one of the most enjoyable trips Fred and I had made, and we are both going to come back.

7

Further Tales Of
The Miramichi

We had such a wonderful time fishing for salmon on the Miramichi that first trip that we went back again the next year. When I got there, I found that the guide whom I had liked so much, Joe Case, had died. I felt very sad. They assigned a new guide to me, a young man about eighteen years old named Fred Green. He was a character. He knew the river like nobody else, and he was so eager to do things for you.

Oftentimes, Fred and I would stop on shore for a shore lunch. Fred would prepare a meal that was out of this world. Wonderful food and it was always tea, no coffee. I drank so much tea up there that when I got back home, I couldn't even think of another cup of tea, I was so anxious to get coffee again. Freddie stuck with me and he taught me a lot about salmon and places on the river to look for salmon. Eventually, he went on to be a conservation officer from St. John. And, later on, he headed up a department in the St. John Canadian Fisheries

Division.

One day, Freddie said to me, "Tomorrow morning, we're going to float down in the canoe to Doaktown. It's an all day trip and we'll have to leave early in the morning." Pearlie had one of the other guides take a truck down to Doaktown that night to meet us. We left in the morning and drifted down all the way to Doaktown. It was there I found the shop of one of the premier salmon fly tiers in Canada, Wallace Doak.

I went into his shop and introduced myself, and Wallace and I talked for a long time about tying flies. I soon found that he lived up to his reputation of being a premier salmon fly tier. We exchanged some flies, and I told him about the Knowles Butterfly and left him a couple. His young son, Jerry Doak, was in the shop with him learning to tie flies.

Hans Lange's first salmon on a fly rod

Altogether, I spent about an hour talking with them and learning about the salmon flies they used on the Miramichi, and the techniques they used to tie them. Today, Jerry Doak is also considered one of the premier fly tiers of the North American continent, following in his father's footsteps. He is featured in a wonderful book just published called *The Atlantic Salmon Fly* by Judith Dunham which features salmon flies and premier fly tiers from all over the world. His father, Wallace Doak, tied a beautiful salmon fly with gorgeous feathers that was a work of art. He gave me some and I bought a few. I still have his flies. I never used them. I intended to frame them. All these years have gone by and I still haven't gotten to it. I will put them in one of those shadow boxes and hang them up on the wall. They are absolutely beautiful.

We had wonderful fishing the second year, even better than the first. I think the food was better the second year as well. We had lobster dinners and some were almost gourmet.

The following year when I went up to the Miramichi, Freddie Green had been appointed a conservation officer. Although he was no longer guiding for money, he still came to camp to renew old acquaintances. He asked me if I would take another trip with him down the river just for the heck of it, and maybe see how a conservation officer works. "It'll be a lot of fun," Freddie said, "and why don't you bring a couple of bottles of that Crown Royale just for old time sake."

We had been at Pearlie's two or three days and the fishing had been pretty good. So I said, "Okay, Freddie. I'll take a day off and go with you."

Now the way that guides fish the Miramichi is to hang a chain out the rear end of the canoe. They pick a spot at the head of a salmon pool, throw this chain out, and pull the canoe there while the sport sits in the front and fishes across on both sides

51

and facing downriver. When you fish facing downriver like that, you can't see anyone coming from behind you unless you turn around. But, of course, you would never be looking that way, you would always be looking down stream. Well, Fred decided that he would represent me as an official from St. John that day.

So we floated down the river and when we saw someone fishing, we would pull up along side and ask to see their fishing license. Were they ever surprised to see someone there and especially a conservation officer! And, we were surprised also to find out how many were fishing without a license.

Whenever we found somebody without a license, Fred would point at me and say, "This is my supervisor from St. Johns. Whatever decision he makes about your not having a license, I will go along with."

Freddie had a badge and uniform and everything that game wardens needed up there in Canada to make their job official. I was just in a fishing outfit but I would talk to the sport. Some would get tears in their eyes because they were out there fishing for food for the family. I would pat them on the back and say, "Well, if you promise that the first time you get some money, you'll go and buy a fishing license, I'll buy you a drink right here and now. And you won't get a ticket for not having a license."

They all agreed that as soon as they got off the river, they would go to the hardware or the fishing store and get a license. Then I would reach down for a bottle of that Crown Royale, and pour everyone a shot right then and there.

We checked a good many canoes on the way down, and by the time we got to Doaktown, both bottles of that Crown Royale were empty, and Freddie and I were feeling pretty good. We gave a lot of people who lived along the Miramichi River a real boost that day. They all thought they were going to be arrested and none of them were. They wound up with a good drink of whiskey instead—Crown Royale whiskey—and if there is anything better in the world, I don't know what it is. By God, it's the nectar of the gods.

At the end of the day, we finally got to Doaktown. It was a darned good thing we had a sober driver to help load that canoe on a truck and drive us back to camp. We couldn't get to bed quick enough when we got there either. We didn't even wait for dinner. But that was a memorable day.

No story about fishing for salmon on the Miramichi would be complete without telling about a practical joke that I pulled on Freddie Glass that backfired on me. Freddie and I would always have breakfast together before taking off for the day's fishing, and everyday we made a dollar bet as to who would catch the best fish that day. Every day it seemed like Freddie was beating me.

Well, this day, Joe Case, my guide, said to me, "John, I'm going to take you way up stream to a little pool that's hardly ever fished. I'm pretty sure there's a big salmon in there." So Joe and I poled up stream in the canoe until we came to this beautiful bend in the river. Joe had all the pools named and I don't remember ever fishing that particular hole before that morning.

I started fishing while Joe pulled the canoe up on shore and beached it. I had a couple of good salmon on and lost them, and then I hooked into one that I was able to land. Joe went downstream and tailed it for me, and brought it back to where we had the canoe stashed on the rocks. It was a beautiful fish, a male salmon, bright, and it was about sixteen pounds.

I looked at that salmon a long time and I said "Joe, I want to keep this fish because this will beat whatever Fred can catch today. I want to take it back to camp with us."

Joe looked at me and said, "You want to win that bet real bad, don't you, John?"

I said, "I would like to beat that old guy if I can."

Joe smiled and said, "Well, I will show you how to do it, John." He took a long stick and started pushing rocks and small stones down that fish's mouth. I don't know how many rocks and stones he pushed down that salmon's throat, but there must have been twenty or thirty. He pushed them way down inside the fish's gullet. When I picked the fish up, I knew that it had gained about ten pounds. I laughed and thought what a great time we will have when we get back to camp with this.

When we got back to camp that night, Fred was waiting with his guide and he was all smiles and he said, "Well, John I really beat you today, I got a beaut." He held up this fish and we put it on the back of a canoe that we had pulled out of the water. We got the tape and measured it. Then, I brought my fish out and I laid it down alongside his. Those two salmon were like brothers. There wasn't a tenth of an inch difference in the length of them.

I shook my head at Fred and said, "I know I got you beat Fred because even though my salmon's the same length as yours, mine is a bigger fish, a healthier fish, and a better fish. So we will weigh them to sees who wins the buck."

Well, Fred's salmon weighed approximately sixteen pounds and mine weighed nearly twenty-four. He scratched his head and looked at that fish of mine, and picked it up and hefted it a dozen times and he kept shaking his head. He just couldn't believe it. I said, "There's no question about who caught the better fish. So pay me the buck you owe me."

We went into dinner that night, and I laughed and kidded Fred about it all during supper and afterwards, about how much better a fisherman I was than he was.

As I said before, we made boxes and shipped these fish back in ice and moss.

We shipped a box of fish back the next day with that fish in it. When we got back to Detroit, we decided to have a salmon dinner for some of our friends from Ford Motor Company. Executives whom we had been doing business with, and who knew all about the trip we had taken. We decided to have the dinner at Sammy Suffrin's Wonder Bar on Washington Boulevard in Detroit. It was a hangout of ours and we spent a lot of time there. When we arranged this salmon dinner, Fred called me in the afternoon. He said, "Don't you worry about the fish. I'll go to the locker and get them. How many fish do you think we need?"

I said, "Bring about six salmon at least because those guys are going to like it, and they are going to eat it like it was going out of style."

"Okay." he said. "Don't worry about it. I'll go to the locker and I'll get the fish and I'll clean them myself."

We never cleaned the salmon that we shipped home; we only gilled them, because if you took only the gills out, the salmon would stay fresh much longer. So these fish were all stored in the locker with just the gills removed and none of them were opened up.

That night we had the dinner. We were seated at the table. The waiters were waiting on us hand and foot bringing drinks, appetizers and salads. The table was laid out with sterling silver, fine china and crystal glass. It was like a king's banquet. Finally, it came time to serve the salmon. Soon everybody except me had been served. I finally grabbed a waiter and said, "What the heck is going on here? Everybody's been served but me."

The waiter said, "We're bringing your portion right now,

sir."

Finally one of the waiters brought me a plate covered with a napkin. When I saw that napkin I knew what was coming to me. I took the napkin off and there were those rocks. Fred had found them in that fish and had washed them and brought them down and put them on my plate. There was a note lying on top the rocks that said, "You lying so and so. I not only want my dollar back but I want you to get up and tell these friends of ours what a crook you are."

By that time, everybody was staring at me. So I had to stand up and read that note. I'll never get over that. Out of all the salmon we had sent back, that night Fred picked out the one that Joe Case and I had filled with rocks to win the dollar bet.

Well, everybody kidded and joked with me about that. I put those rocks in a bag and brought them home. I still have them to this day. Why I kept them I don't know. A rock's a rock. I don't think if Fred had tried to pick out that particular fish he could have found it in all those other salmon. We had sent back about seventy-four. And, what was even more embarrassing to me, was that I ended up buying Fred another fish knife to replace the one he had broken cleaning that salmon!

8

Prairie Dogs And Antelope

Starting in the late 1950's, Freddie Glass and I began taking combination hunting and fishing trips all over the country. We went out west to Yellowstone, New Brunswick, and British Columbia, to name a few. On one particular trip, we went to Wyoming.

There were five of us in the party. We drove our car through Chicago all the way to Wyoming. We had arrangements to stay with an outfitter who had a ranch near Gillespie. He owned about twenty thousand acres of land with three or four beautiful trout streams. We would hunt in the morning and fish in the afternoon. He had a beautiful house for his ranch hands way back in about fifteen miles from the road. We stayed there for the three weeks we spent on his ranch. It was on a high point of a hill surrounded by a fence. We could stand along the edge of that fence on that hill, and take a pair of binoculars, and look out over the valleys and see game all over the place.

We went out there primarily to hunt deer and antelope, and, of course, everybody got a mule deer and an antelope. There were so many of them. I can remember while driving through that Wyoming country that the prairie seemed alive with antelope. Herds of them running along each side of the road. Our guides and the rancher would take us out in jeeps, and they would position us in an area and then drive back to the ranch house and leave us there for half a day or a day. Sometimes, we would take food with us; sometimes the guides would come out and get us for lunch.

The place teemed with wild animals. It was no trouble at all to kill a big mule deer. Of course, we all wanted a big rack, so we held off a long time and looked at a lot of animals.

I got my mule deer early on, and had it taken back to camp, cleaned and hung up on the meat pole. Then I wanted to get a real nice antelope head to mount. So the rancher dropped me off in an area all by myself, and said, "This should be a good spot. I've seen a lot of good bucks here. And, if you take your time and pick one out, you'll be able to get the kind of a head you want."

I was using a .270 rifle that I had made and scoped. It was just about as accurate at 150 yards as any gun I ever owned. I started walking and I walked around for a long time, up and down hills, watching those antelope. I could see a lot of them. It was just a matter of picking out the one I wanted. Finally, I saw the buck. He had about nine-ten inch horns on him and that's pretty good size for an antelope.

In order to get into position to shoot, I had to crawl a ways through the sage brush. I got into position on my knees and then into a crouch. But, when I went to squat down on my rump to shoot, I sat right on some prickly pear cactuses. Wow! I gave a jump and fell over backwards and sat right down on that cactus plant again. I just filled my backside with those cactus needles. They went through my clothes and my pants, and were embedded in my behind like porcupine quills. I dropped my pants and struggled to reach the quills while I danced all over the place. It hurt like hell, and I couldn't see to get the damn things out.

I was still hopping and dancing around when the rancher came along. He had a good laugh at my expense and then took me back to camp and gave me a big mirror and a pair of tweezers. I sat the mirror on the floor and spent the next two days bending over it, pulling out cactus barbs. I never did get them all out, and I still have some today I think. It ended my hunting for a couple of days. I was the sorriest guy in the world.

Well, we all got our bucks and our antelope, and we had two or three extra days to fool around. There was a place way back on the ranch where I had seen a prairie dog town. There were mounds and mounds of prairie dogs hills for a mile or so, with literally thousands of prairie dogs sitting out on the mounds. For some reason, I had brought my .22 rifle with me, thinking it would be perfect to use to shoot some prairie dogs. That afternoon, I decided to go back and spend some time shooting prairie dogs. The guy who owned the ranch said that he would actually pay me to go back there and kill the dogs.

So I pussyfooted through this prairie dog town and found a big knoll and sat down on it. I started to shoot at prairie dogs with the twenty-two. I killed quite a few of them, and after I had been there a half or three quarters of an hour, I heard something buzzing. I looked down at my feet and there were a couple of huge rattlesnakes lying there. It scared the devil out of me. I jumped up and started shooting at those snakes. I must have shot at them ten or more times before I hit one, I was so shook up. I had an automatic twenty-two Winchester. I don't know how many shells I had in it, but I had quite a few.

I finally killed both snakes and I looked around, and there were rattlesnakes all over the place. I could go to almost any prairie dog hole and there would be a rattlesnake sitting at the mouth of it.

I picked those two snakes up. One had seven rattles on it; the other had nine. They were fearsome-looking snakes. I pussyfooted my way back out of that prairie dog town. I got out to the edge of it and walked all the way back to the ranch. When I got there my guide, one of the cowboys, started laughing when he saw the two snakes I was carrying.

The rancher said, "Didn't you know that every prairie dog hole has a rattlesnake or two in it? They get along real good together."

I said, "I didn't know that, but I know it now. And I'm not going back there for any reason!"

He said, "Well you're lucky you didn't get bitten by one of them. I should have cautioned you about the rattlesnakes when you went back there. You give me those two snakes and I'll skin them out for you. I'll tan them and make a band for that Stetson hat you bought back in town the other day."

He was true to his word and made a hat band out of those snake skins. On the way in, we had stopped in town and bought a bunch of western shirts and hats and God knows what. He put the one with the nine rattles on my hat, and he put the other skin on one of my friends' hats. When I came back from that trip with all the meat and heads and the hat with the snakeskin on it, my wife just about flipped. She didn't like that hat at all. I had that hat for a long time, but I didn't wear it because it looked crazy for me to be wearing a western hat around East Lansing with a rattlesnake hide on it. So one time later when I was down at the race track, I gave the hat to one of my trainers. It fit him quite well and he wore it for a long time. He was proud as hell of that hat with a real rattlesnake skin on it with those rattles.

I'll never forget that trip. It was really something to be shook up like that—standing in a field of not only hundreds of prairie dogs but thousands of rattlesnakes. I didn't want any more of that. I certainly never went back there to shoot more prairie dogs!

9

Of Moose And Men
Part One

I have made many combination moose hunting and fishing trips with my friends and I have made seven or eight to Canada. The first trip was to a place called Blind River north of Sault Ste Marie in the Canadian shield country. My friends and I made contact with an outfitter in Canada who had a float plane, and he flew us two or three hundred miles into the bush to a secluded lake. The pilot dropped us off with a couple of canoes and all our duffel. We stayed there for two or three weeks, moose hunting and fishing.

The outfitter would fly our guides in with tents, equipment and food two or three days before we got there. They would have everything set up for us when we landed on the lake and taxied up to the campsite. It was a wonderful adventure each time. There were many exciting incidents that I recall. I really fell in love with those moose hunting and fishing expeditions.

Napoleon Vincent

It was a wonderful way to hunt from a canoe—leisurely, no sweat. We would paddle up lakes and rivers for miles. We would pole over numerous beaver dams until we came to another small lake. There, we would get out of the canoe and conceal ourselves on the shore, and the guide would get out his birch bark moose caller and try to call in a bull moose. I never had an unsuccessful trip. I don't know how many moose I shot, but I shot some really big ones.

On four of the trips I took up there, I had the same Indian guide. His name was Napoleon Vincent, and his knowledge of the woods was uncanny. Napoleon was a good companion and guide. We would take a canoe in the morning and paddle up different rivers and around different lakes until about ten or eleven. Then we would make a shore lunch. We spent the afternoons fishing. Those lakes were absolutely teeming with big pike, and we caught many of them.

Our Indian guides would fillet those fish and cook them. They would roll them in pancake flour and fry them, and we would sit around the fire at night and eat these delicious fillets until they were coming out our ears. I could never get enough of that fish. I have memories of eating so much some nights that I was actually ill with stomach cramps.

Now, when you spend hours and days alone with an Indian guide in a canoe, you get to know a lot about him. None of these Indian guides were very talkative. But by prodding you could get stories from them that were always interesting. Napoleon could always tell stories because he had been guiding for a long time. Unfortunately, he was killed in Blind River in an auto accident about four years after I met him.

It was Napoleon who taught me how to call moose. I asked him one day if he would teach me. He thought it over for a moment. "Okay," he said. "But, it not easy and big bull moose nothing to fool around with."

That night he made me a moose caller out of birch bark that he cut from a tree. He fashioned it into a horn and put the white side of the birch on the inside. I sat around that night and blew that moose caller until my face turned red. Napoleon would blow a call and then I would take the horn and blow one. Napoleon would shake his head, and then I would blow it again trying to imitate his call. This went on for hours, and Napoleon got a good laugh as did everybody else over my feeble attempts to sound like a bull moose.

But I didn't give up. Every night I would take that horn and start blowing. Some nights it even scared away the bears that hung around the camp. Then one night, the squeal turned into the full-throated bellow of a bull moose ready to challenge the world. That was very gratifying.

Now, nothing would satisfy me until I tried that darn thing out to see if it would bring in a moose. We had a wonderful fish dinner that night. The guides had filleted all these big pike and we ate fish until it came out our ears. After dinner, we sat around for a few minutes. It was a beautiful night, there was no wind, it was quiet, it was warm, the moon was about half full, and I thought this is the perfect night to try my moose call.

I took my rifle and put it in the front of a canoe, and I pushed the canoe out and paddled down the river alone to where there was a big moose crossing. When I say "big moose crossing," I mean there were thousands of tracks across the river. It was uncanny how moose can find a place like that on a river and know just where to go to cross. It was quiet and peaceful and there was no noise in the woods. I pulled the canoe up on shore and sat in it. I heard nothing in the woods so I picked up the moose caller and blew a couple of bellows. Right across the river about a mile away, a moose answered me! I thought, "Boy, am I good with this machine. I'll give it another blow and see what happens."

It's really something to hear when a bull moose is on the prowl, and hears an antagonistic moose bellowing from across the river at him. It's like asking him whether he's chicken or not, or whether he wants to come out and fight like a man. So, I blew the moose horn a couple more times, and this big bull from across the river kept answering. Then I heard him coming through those woods a mile away, breaking brush and trees like match sticks. He sounded like a freight train coming through those woods.

There was nobody around me, nobody near me, and I sat there and listened to this huge animal coming to look for the guy that said he couldn't fight. The closer he got to me, the more I wondered what I was doing there. Pretty soon the hair began to rise on the back of my neck.

I reached for the moose horn again but thought better of it. "To hell with that," I thought. "I've had enough of this crap. That big sunovagun is going to come right out of that woods across from me and right through this moose crossing. The water is only waist deep here. If he comes across that water, he'd be pretty damn close to me. I'll have one shot and if I don't drop him, I'll be done for."

I launched the canoe into the river and paddled a little downstream and waited for him to show up. When he did, he was madder than hell. His neck was straight up and he was looking for the guy that said he couldn't fight. He plunged right into the water after me and he looked bigger than an elephant.

I laid to with the paddle and got the hell out of there. I think the backwash from the wake of my canoe must have slowed him down. I never looked back. "So much for moose calling," I thought. I could feel the hair on the back of my neck standing up. When I got back, I sheepishly told Napoleon what happened.

Napoleon said, "You foolish go out there alone. Never go out alone. Always take a guide with you to back you up."

I don't know why he would say that because the guides aren't allowed to carry guns. The only thing a guide carries is a double-bitted ax, and it's with him day and night. He sleeps with it, eats with it, and carries it with him every second. And, for the life of me, I don't know what Napoleon would have done with just an ax against that monster.

10

Of Moose And Men
Part Two

After my experience with moose calling, I decided that I had better stick with my guide on any future trips looking for moose. It became a practice of mine to sight in my rifle so that when I shot at an animal I knew exactly where and how far my shot would go. One year, I went to Canada with a friend, Ed Pierce, an engineer who worked for Chevrolet in Flint. Ed heard how I could make long distance shots with considerable accuracy, and he was always kidding me about it. It was all just good natured fun and fellowship between us.

This one morning, Napoleon and I took off toward the other end of the lake from where we were camped. About two, two and a half miles up the lake, we found a stream and we followed that up river quite a ways. Now one thing about Canadian rivers and streams is that there is a beaver dam about every half mile or so. When we came to a beaver dam, we would get out and pull the canoe over and paddle for another half a mile to the next dam. We did that sixteen times that day until we came to where the river ran out of another lake. It was a wild spot with many moose signs around, a lot of moose crossings, and it looked like good country to hunt.

We pulled up on the shore of the lake near a bunch of blow downs, and I stretched down behind these logs and tried to get into a position where I could shoot if I saw anything. I had a clear view across the lake. It was about two hundred and fifty yards to the other shore, and it would be a long shot if I saw a moose. But, I thought it was a shot I could make, if I got a good clear target. Anyway, I hunkered down there with Napoleon and just waited to see what was going to happen. After about a half hour, Napoleon got tired of waiting and got up and said, "Well, I'll sashay up through the bushes and see if I can see any moose sign."

He left and I sat another half an hour or so and didn't see anything. Finally, directly across from me on the other side of the lake, I saw this big bull moose come out. He walked out into the edge of the lake and started munching lily pads. I pulled down on him with my gun and compensated for the yardage. I touched the trigger off, and he dropped like somebody hit him on the head with a hammer. I never saw a moose go down so fast or so hard. And, you know he just kicked a couple of times when he hit the water and he was as stone dead as anything could be. Napoleon heard the shot and came running back.

"What did you shoot at?" he asked. He looked out across the lake but couldn't see anything because that moose was so far away on the other side of the lake.

"I got a moose."

"Where, where?" he asked.

I said, "Let's get in the canoe and cross the lake."

"You shoot that far? I can't believe it."

I said, "Yeah, I think I killed him."

Napoleon looked at me, not believing what I was telling him. "With just one shot?" he said. "That far?"

So we paddled across the lake and sure enough the moose was there and he was a dandy too. We cut his legs off at the knees and quartered him out. I kept the head and the cape and put that in the front of the canoe, and we had these four quarters of moose yet to load. We distributed them evenly along the bottom of the canoe and then set out for camp.

Along the way were the sixteen beaver dams that we had crossed to get there in the first place. Every time we pulled that heavily loaded canoe over a dam, we were afraid we were going to tear the bottom out of it, snagging it on a log or a limb or something. It was real tough, hard work.

We finally got back to the lake where our camp was, and we still had two and a half miles to go down the lake. By that time, it was about five o'clock in the afternoon, and the wind had started to come up and we were headed right into it. It was real tough paddling. Not only that, but we only had an inch of free board on that damn canoe. If either of us moved too much or pushed the paddles too hard, water would come over the side of the canoe.

The further we got out into that lake, the rougher it got and the stronger the wind blew. The waves were piling up ahead of us and the canoe was threatening to swamp at any second. I finally called back to Napoleon, "Can you swim?" And, he called back, "No, I can't swim at all. Never could swim." I couldn't believe it. An Indian not knowing how to swim. But, then I looked at those waves and I wondered if anyone could swim in that stuff.

I yelled back at Napoleon, "What about the moose meat?

Will that sink or float if we turn over?"

He yelled over the wind, "It'll go down like a rock right to the bottom." The waves were getting higher and higher. They were slapping over the sides of the canoe and we were taking on water pretty fast.

I shouted at Napoleon, "The only thing to do is to keep heading the way we are and back paddle. We'll back paddle this goddamn canoe back to that little island that we passed half way up here. If we get back to that island, we'll pull up there and wait for the wind to die down so we can get back to camp."

Napoleon shouted back, "We can try." But he looked doubtful that we would make it. We very cautiously paddled backwards with the canoe loaded to the gunnels with moose meat and the wind blowing like mad. The wind helped us go backwards but it was touch and go for quite a while.

We finally made it to the tiny island. We pulled the canoe up and beached it, and we sat there for five hours before the wind died down. It was after nine o'clock that night when it finally subsided enough for us to get in that canoe and paddle that thing back. Even then I could see the lake water coming over the side of the canoe. It couldn't help coming over once in a while, but if it got so it poured over we would be in a panic situation. We had to be careful the whole way.

As a finale to this story, we got the meat back to the camp, and while we were sitting around telling our stories I was bragging about what a long wonderful shot I had made. This guy Pierce is kidding me about exaggerating and that nobody could hit a moose at two hundred and fifty yards with a .270. We had a lot of fun that night talking and kidding about my prowess with a rifle.

The next morning before we went out, Ed made plans to go back to the same lake where I had been the day before. He asked a lot of questions about how we got there, where I was, and where I was sitting when I shot the moose.

To make a long story short, when he came in that night, he shook my hand and said, "John, I want to tell you something. We went up to that lake where you were yesterday, and I found the very log you sat behind and shot. Here's your empty shell. We could only find the one. We got in the canoe and went straight across the lake. It's not two hundred and fifty yards. It's a helluva lot closer to three hundred yards, and we saw where you cut the legs off the moose and skinned him out. I take my hat off to you. That was the most remarkable shot I've ever seen. I sure want to congratulate you."

Of course, I very meekly said, "Oh that was nothing. I do that all the time."

One day, Napoleon said to me, "I'm going to take you way back to a beaver dam tomorrow. Big beaver meadow back there off the other shore."

I said, "Napoleon, how do you know there's a big beaver meadow back there? Have you ever been in this territory before?"

Napoleon shook his head no and said, "I have never hunted off this island before. But I know there is a big beaver meadow back there on the mainland."

I said, "If you've never been back there, how in the world do you know that there's a meadow back in there?"

Napoleon just shrugged his shoulders and said, "Well, I just know. You come tomorrow morning. We go back to it."

The next morning, we paddled the canoe from the island to the mainland, and we took off through the woods. He was in the lead and I was trying to keep up with him. It was about three or four miles back. Finally, he stopped and said, "Be real quiet because we're coming to the moose meadow now and I don't want to scare anything away."

We crept up the last quarter of a mile, walking like two Indians. We got up on a big rock on the edge of a pretty little green meadow. It was a great big low spot tucked in the hills with moose tracks all over the place. We sat there an hour and we didn't talk or move. Finally, Napoleon touched me on the knee and pointed across the meadow and said, "Here he comes Johnnie, and he's a big one."

I looked over to my left from that rock, and the most tremendous bull moose I ever saw walked slowly out of the woods to cross that beaver meadow right in front of us. He was about a hundred and twenty-five yards away from me. I had an excellent rest for my rifle on that rock, and when he got in the middle of that beaver meadow, I shot. The animal, which was huge and black, and had such an immense rack of horns, just kept on walking as though nothing had happened.

Napoleon says, "You missed. Shoot again."

I racked another shell into the chamber. I still had an excellent shot at him. I aimed again and pulled the trigger but that moose kept right on walking.

Napoleon shook his head in disbelief and shouted, "Shoot! Shoot! Shoot!"

I racked a third shell into the chamber and fired just as he disappeared from the edge of the beaver meadow. I knew I missed with that shot because I saw the bark fly from the bushes in back of him.

Napoleon was fit to be tied. We sat there for about five or ten minutes. He insisted on waiting because if the moose had fallen down, then it would have a chance to stiffen up before we went down there and would not charge us. If you walk up on these bull moose too soon and they're still alive, they'll take after you like a dog. They can do a lot of damage to a guy if they get to him.

So we waited and waited, and finally we started down around the edge of the forest. Napoleon started whacking the flat side of his double bitted ax against trees as he went by to show his frustration at my shooting. He made those trees ring like a bell every time he hit one. I was downhearted as well; I couldn't imagine how I could miss on shots like that. Napoleon would go two or three feet, and he would take that ax and swing it against a tree. The ring of it was almost deafening.

We walked on down through the meadow and the back of the willows where the moose had stood was all splattered with blood. I knew then that I had hit the animal. We tracked him as far as we could with the blood, and then we lost track of him so we started to circle. But, we couldn't find him.

Indian guides with my sister, Dorie, in Canada

About that time, my partner and his Indian guide showed up on the edge of the beaver meadow. They had heard the shooting from camp, and they got in the canoe and followed us. His Indian guide followed our track s right up to where we were.

We spread out and started to make circles in the direction the moose had gone. Shortly thereafter, I heard a gun shot. They had found my moose up in the woods with his tremendous rack resting over a big log. When we got there and looked, you could have seen that thing for a country mile. It was so big and shiny and yellow that it was impossible not to see. We looked the animal over, and I have never seen anything so big. We had a tape with us and measured it. It was 68½ inches from point to point. After I got home, I got a Boone and Crockett medal for the animal, and I was listed in the Boone and Crockett hunting file.

The Indian guides started to skin the animal out. I told them I wanted that head and cape because I wanted to have it mounted. But, I didn't know how we were going to get it out of there, because it was three and one half miles to camp. My friend's Indian guide was just a little guy about five foot five and he says, "I can carry that thing out."

I said, "If you can carry that head and cape out to the canoe, I will give you fifty dollars." He agreed.

We finished skinning the animal out and cut it all up. My wife had made a whole bunch of gunny sacks out of bed sheets for just such an occasion as this. So we boned the meat and put it in the gunny sacks. The idea was that the gunny sacks kept the flies from the meat and protected it.

We filled all the gunny sacks I had with me, and we started the four of us carrying all that meat out to the canoes. I never worked so hard in all my life. I remember that little Indian guide carrying that cape and head. It took all three of us to put that thing on his shoulders. He put a tumpline around his head, and he had to go sideways through the trees so that he could get those immense horns through without knocking himself down. He carried that head out to the river and out to the canoe without stopping once. His stamina was absolutely amazing.

It took us about two days, and I mean two *full* days of making trips to the canoes and back with the meat. I wanted to have the hide too but it was too heavy to carry, and if we had cut it up, it wouldn't have been any good. I always regret leaving that beautiful moose hide in the woods back there by that beaver meadow but, it was so far from the river, we decided not to carry it out.

It was a wonderful trip though, and we had that moose on the back of our car on the way home, and we had so many people come over to look at it and ask us where we got it, and admire it. It was one of the most successful moose hunting trips I ever had, and it was without question the biggest moose I've ever seen.

11

Goldilocks And The Three Bears—Canadian Style

My friend, Ed Bligh, had been going to Batchawanna Bay in Ontario, way the heck and gone up in the north country of Canada. He had been there several times to fish and hunt, but I had never been that far north in Canada.

We talked about taking a trip up there one year. Ed found a young pilot with a float plane to take us with our equipment to a remote island in the middle of Batchawanna Bay—a place where nobody had ever been before as far as we knew. We made arrangements with the pilot to come back in a week's time and pick us up.

We drove up to Canada and put our stuff in the airplane and he flew us to this island. It was a large place, about three and a half miles long. The pilot helped us put up our tent at the edge of the water and dropped off a canoe. Then we were ready to enjoy a week's fishing completely isolated by ourselves, and away from all the worries of civilization out there in the middle of that Canadian wilderness.

"I'll be back in a week," he said. "Have fun."

The first thing Ed and I did was to jump in the canoe and paddle out into the bay and start catching fish. The fish were easy to get along with, and soon we had a stringer of good sized pike. Ed was stringing up a pike when he looked back at the camp site. "Hey John," he said. "Look at the goddamn bears at our tent."

There were three bears rummaging around in our equipment and around the tent and turning everything upside down. I grabbed a paddle and shouted at Ed, "We better get back there before we lose everything."

Ed picked up a paddle and we paddled as fast as we could back to the campsite. "What are we gonna do when we get there?" Ed asked. "Those bears look pretty bold." We hit the beach running, waving our arms and yelling at the top of our voices. The bears spooked pretty easy when they saw us and ran off in the woods.

After we settled down, we cleaned the fish on a couple of rocks by the water and then cooked supper. Somehow, I felt uneasy about the whole thing. We weren't allowed to bring a gun into Canada, and if those bears came back there wouldn't be much we could do about it.

After supper I said to Ed, "Let's be sure we hang everything up out of reach of those bears in case they come back in the night. If we don't do that, we could lose all our food. It'll be a good thing to keep everything hanging up in case they raid us while we're fishing."

We settled down for the night and snugged ourselves in. It had been a long day and I was tired. I dropped off to sleep but not for long. Ed rolled over and shook me awake, "Do you hear that?" he said.

sniffing around the tent. We stuck our heads out the tent door, and sure enough there were three bears parading around in the moonlight. We hollered at them again and they took off on the run.

We went back to sleep only to be awakened again in a few minutes. Again, we yelled at them. Again they ran away. This whole thing kept repeating itself. We would go back to sleep. They would come back. We would yell. They would run away. We would go back to sleep. They would come back. We would yell.

Finally, I said to Ed, "We're never gonna get any sleep this way. Let's get up and build a fire and hope that keeps them away." That fire changed everything in the darkness. We felt a little more secure. But, we knew the bears were out there just watching and waiting for us to let down our guard.

About dawn, we made breakfast and hung everything back up in the trees. When daylight came, we saw the bears had eaten all the fish we had cleaned the night before. We had left the fillets on a rock by the shore, and the bears had cleaned those up as slick as anything. "Well, we might as well go fishing," Ed grumbled. "That's what to hell we came here for."

So, off we went fishing. We hadn't paddled far from the campsite before we saw those bears come back and start moseying around the tent. We paddled back to shore and chased them away again. But this time, they didn't scare as easily as they did before. They snarled at us and backed up very slowly. Two of them were good sized, about three hundred pounds or more. The third was a cub of about a hundred and twenty-five pounds.

That went on all day long. We had to either stay at the campsite or else put up with the bears tearing into everything we had, looking for food. Each time we chased them away, they got a little more aggressive with us.

"My God," Ed said. "We're never going to get any fishing done like this. I don't think we scare them too much any more. Pretty soon they'll be chasing us away from the camp."

"Yeah," I said. "I think the best thing to do is to hang a white towel out on a limb, and hope like hell that bush pilot comes along and sees it. This could get pretty rough on us if we don't get out of here pretty soon."

It was getting late in the day but we hung the towel out anyway. Not one airplane came over. Night was coming on and I wondered how we could keep those bears away without staying up all night again. I was already tired from lack of sleep from the night before.

Ed looked at me and smiled weakly. He pointed at one of the bears sitting at the edge of our campsite. "See that big black one there—the one sitting there licking his chops—I think he's measuring you up for supper tonight."

"Maybe we should throw him a fish," I said.

We crawled into our sleeping bags, and tried to settle down for the night. But it wasn't for long. I heard something grunting right next to me outside the tent. One of the bears was right on the other side of the canvas sniffing in my ear.

I jumped up and yelled, "Dammit, you're right, Ed. He wants us for supper." I scrambled outside yelling at the bear at the top of my voice. "Get the hell out of here," I screamed. I grabbed my flashlight and flashed the light in its eyes. It was the big black one Ed had joked about earlier. The light spooked it for a bit and it ran off into the dark. We built a fire and got the flames burning bright so we could see what was going on. Of course, the bears didn't come up there with the flames and the big fire going. We sat up all night keeping the fire burning. In the morning, the bears were there sitting at the edge of the campsite. Now, they were really losing their caution and getting more aggressive, and they didn't run worth a damn the third day we went after them.

We went out to fish again. It was better than sitting in the camp staring back at those bears. But, every time we left, they came into the campsite and started tearing things up. Finally, we had to quit fishing and just stay there and chase them away. "Don't they ever go anywhere else to eat?" Ed asked.

I just shook my head and wished to hell they would go away, especially the big black one, who kept edging in closer and closer to the tent. Now they didn't chase worth a damn. We finally had to keep the fire going all day and all night.

We kept looking at the sky hoping to hear an airplane engine but nothing came by. We knew we would have to spend another sleepless night just keeping those bears away.

The next morning was the same thing. Those bears just sat out there waiting for us to go fishing. We just sat there staring back at them. My eyes felt like they had a ton of gravel under the lids from staying awake three nights in a row.

Then, late in the afternoon, we heard an airplane motor. Ed and I ran out and hung every white towel we had in the trees around the campsite. We even stood there and yelled and waved our arms. The plane came over and circled around, and then came in for a landing on the lake. It was our bush pilot and he taxied up to us. He stuck his head out the plane window and yelled, "What's the problem? You got troubles?"

I yelled back, "Yeah, we sure as hell do. We got a lot of troubles. And, they're all bear troubles. We want you to take us the hell out of here."

"Okay," he said. "I can see those bears sitting there by your tent. They can be pretty pesky if they think there's food available. Pack up your gear and we'll be on our way."

We loaded up that airplane as fast we could, and as the plane taxied down to the end of the bay, I looked back and saw those three goddamn bears sitting there at the edge of the water, watching us take off like they were sorry to see us go. And, I could swear the big black one was waving his paw at me to come back soon.

12

A Shaggy Hunting Dog Story

Back in the early forties, I did a lot of pheasant hunting. There were plenty of pheasants around to hunt, and it was very easy to go out and get a limit of four roosters in a day if you had a good bird dog. I liked to hunt with a dog because I love to see a dog work, and I love to see him retrieve. Because of that, I bought a hunting dog from a fellow down south. It was a comanche pointer, and the guy had pretty well trained it before I bought it. However, I felt the dog needed more training than it had. It was a real sleek dog with all the fine lines of its ancestry, and when it went on point it was like a picture.

I took the dog around and showed him to some of my hunting friends. And, one in particular, Vic Demarco, liked the dog very much.

"Gosh, John," he said. "I'd like to buy that dog. How much you want for him?"

"Three hundred dollars," I said.

Vic shook his head. "No way. At that price that thing would have to be the best hunting dog in the world. And, I don't think I ever heard of a comanche pointer." Well, three hundred dollars was not a bad price for a good hunting dog. I knew the dog was worth it. Also, Vic's remark about the best hunting dog in the world bothered me. It made me feel like I was trying to take advantage of a friend.

I knew a fellow in Saginaw that raised pheasants and trained bird dogs with them. He would take the dogs out and teach them to retrieve and work a bird by releasing a live pheasant. I took the dog to him three months before bird season, and he promised to have the dog finished by opening day.

When opening day came, a hunting friend of mine from East Lansing and I drove up to Saginaw to pick up the dog. From there we would go and do some pheasant hunting and see how this dog really worked. When we got there, the dog trainer only shook his head. "Oh," he said. "Your dog's okay, John. He's doing everything I asked him to. He's retrieving and handling well. But I've had a piece of bad luck."

He took us out back where he kept the pheasants in hundred yard long pens. He called them fly pens, and had them chuck full of birds. The trainer took us over to one of these pens, and it was littered with dead cock pheasants. He pointed at all the dead roosters. "Weasels did that," he said. "Somehow they got in this pen and went on a killing rampage. There's about a hundred and twenty-five dead roosters in there. Those weasels sure as hell have cost me a lot of money."

I felt sorry for the guy, I could see that maybe his livelihood was at stake. "Can these things be eaten?" I asked.

"Oh sure," he said. "Those damn weasels only bite them through the head once, and then leave them and go on to another bird right away. I guess that's what you call blood lust."

I looked at those beautiful birds and thought it was such as waste. "Well, if they can be eaten," I said, "I'll give you a dollar a piece for them and take them back home and put them in my freezer locker. I've always enjoyed eating wild game."

He looked at me with a smile and said, "John, you've got a deal." He gave me enough tags on wires for all the birds to prove they were pen raised, and I took all those pheasants and put them in the trunk of my car.

I closed the trunk lid and said to my friend. "Bert, you know the limit is four birds apiece and we've got over a hundred and twenty-five birds here. We might as well go back to Lansing and forget about hunting for today."

"Besides," I continued, "I think we can have some fun with the folks back home when we show them all these birds." I was thinking of Vic Demarco in particular.

Back in those days, the drive from Saginaw to Lansing was all on two lane roads and passed through many little towns along the way. About lunch time, we came to the little town of Owosso and Bert and I agreed it would be nice to stop at a bar and catch a hamburger and a glass of beer. Well, as luck would have it, the bar we picked was the meeting place of the Shiawassee Sportsmen Association. It was packed full of pheasant hunters who had been out that opening day, and they were all bragging a blue streak about their luck.

Bert and I edged our way up to the bar and ordered a beer and the bartender asked us, "How did you fellas do?"

"Oh," I said, "We can't complain. We got a few. You have any luck?"

"None whatsoever," he said. "Didn't even see one. But, then I only had an hour or two to hunt. But, I sure would have liked to have got one. Those wild pheasants are pretty good eating."

Well, one thing led to another and I said to him, "Bert and

I had some pretty good luck today. Would you like a couple of pheasants?"

The bartender said, "I would love to have one or two."

I went out to the car, opened the trunk, took out a couple of cock pheasants, brought them into the bar and handed them to him. All these other guys, the hunters who were standing around, saw me do it. One guy in particular came over and said, "I'm the president of this sportsmen's association." He had a suspicious look on his face, and I could see he was curious as to why Bert and I were giving away what he thought was our day's hunt. I didn't think it was any of his business so I thought I would pull his leg a little bit.

"Oh," I said. "Bert and I had pretty good luck today. We got a few more or less."

"Yeah," he said. "The limit's four. Not many of us here today got that. How many did you guys get, anyway?"

I looked him straight in the face without batting an eye and said, "A hundred and twenty-five."

He about choked when I said that. He set his beer down on the counter and stood there looking at me. Then all of sudden, he turned around and started yelling, "You guys hear that? These guys claim they killed a hundred and twenty-five pheasants. What do you think we oughta do to poor sportsmen like these?"

Everybody started crowding around us and shouting at us, telling us what a couple of rebels we were. I looked around for a way out but there wasn't any. Somebody shouted, "Call the conservation officer. Arrest these guys and throw their butts in jail."

"To hell with that," someone else shouted. "Let's beat the crap out of 'em right here."

I looked sideways at Bert. The joke had gone too far. I

didn't think they would believe me now even if I told them how we really got the pheasants. But, by that time, the bartender had called the police and it was a good thing because the situation was getting real nasty. Two cops came in and pulled us out of the group. Bert looked pretty relieved.

"What the hell is going on here?" one of the police asked.

So we told them. I told them how we had hand-raised tags for every bird we had. They took a look at the tags and checked them all over. Then they started laughing. One of them said, "You two guys came pretty close to getting your noses wiped up in there. Why don't you take these birds and just get the hell out of here and don't come back."

We did just that and headed back to Lansing. But, even with that little episode behind us, I still thought it would be fun to pull Vic Demarco's leg. Vic ran a bar which was a pretty popular watering hole in Lansing. So Bert and I stopped there and sure enough he was tending bar.

We ordered a beer and Vic, of course, asked the usual question about how did the hunting go. I was waiting for exactly that question. I took a sip of beer and said casually, "We did pretty well today Vic. We got a hundred and twenty-five pheasants."

"Yeah," he said. "And, my grandmother shot a bull elephant in her back yard this morning."

He wiped up an imaginary spot on the bar and then walked away laughing. He poured some drinks for a couple of other guys at the other end of the bar. "You hear what those two white hunters are claiming?" he asked them, pointing at us. They shook their heads no.

Vic shouted back at us, "Hey John, tell them how many pheasants you and Bert got today."

Again, I said with a straight face and real casual. "Hundred and twenty-five, wasn't it Bert?"

"Yeah, that was my count," Bert said.

Vic came back and stared at us. "You guys are serious aren't you?" I shrugged my shoulders.

"You had that new dog with you, didn't you? That comanche pointer or whatever it was." I took another drink of beer and smiled at Vic.

"You guys are serious for sure, aren't you?"

"C'mon out to the car, Vic. If you want a half dozen or so, I'll be glad to give them to you."

"Well, I'll be damned," Vic said.

Vic followed us to the car and I opened up the deck lid. His eyes bugged right out when he saw all those rooster pheasants. "Never even got one hen," we said.

"For God sakes," Vic said. "Put that lid back down." He looked all around quickly. "If a conservation officer ever sees that, you guys will go to jail for life."

We walked back into the bar, and I said, "Vic. I'm going to give you six of those birds. I know you hunted hard this morning and didn't get anything. And, it's pretty tough to pheasant hunt without a good bird dog. But, I'm going to reward you with some of those pheasants."

He still couldn't believe it. "How in hell did you guys get so many birds and get away with it?"

I said, "Vic, you never saw a dog work like that dog of mine worked. I don't care how much you ever pay for a dog—you'll never get a dog that works like mine. He's damn near perfect in every respect. He points. He retrieves. He obeys commands left and right. He's really a finished dog."

Vic said, "Well, I gotta have that dog. If he's still for sale, I wanna buy 'em from you. I'll even give you five hundred dollars for him, two hundred more than you asked in the first place."

I said, "You made a deal, ol' buddy. But, I'm not going to overcharge you for the dog. Three hundred was the original asking price and three hundred it is."

"Your one heckuva of friend," Vic said. And, he reached in his pocket and handed me three one hundred dollar bills. I bought the house a round of drinks.

Later on, Bert and I took all those pheasants to a chicken processing plant and had them cleaned and packaged. I gave pheasants away to everybody I knew. I had my freezer full of pheasants for months to come. That was the best opening day of pheasant season I ever had. To see Vic's face when I opened the trunk of my car when he saw all those pheasants was worth a king's ransom to me.

13

The Horse With The Broken Leg

I retired about twenty-five years ago, and between my fishing and hunting, I became interested in horse racing. I guess it was a natural extension of those interests because it was exciting and challenging, and the training of a good thoroughbred race horse under the tutelage of a good trainer required as much savvy and discipline as learning to hunt or fish. It was something that took time to develop, and to watch a horse you own run in a race, and perhaps win, is as thrilling as shooting a trophy moose or catching a lunker fish.

A friend of mine, Doctor Joe Heckert, got me interested in horse racing. We would go to the race track in Detroit on a regular basis—maybe a couple of times a week. The more I went the more I liked it. At first, I only went to watch the races but eventually, I bought two or three thoroughbreds, and kept them stabled at the Detroit Race Course where I could watch them run. It was when I first started going with Joe to the race track that I got a chance to buy my first race horse. I didn't own it long. But it certainly was interesting.

One day, Joe called me and said, "John. An old friend of mine wants to go along with us to the racetrack on Saturday. I hope you don't mind." That friend turned out to be Howard Sober. Howard was a millionaire, most likely a multi-millionaire, and he was a great horse race fan. He owned several thoroughbred horses and loved betting on the races. Howard started to go down with us to Detroit after that first time on a regular basis.

On one particular day on the way down to the track, Howard leaned over from the back seat and said to us, "I have a surprise for you two guys today. I've got a horse running in the seventh race that I know is going to win. If we make a good bet on him, I know we can win some money."

Howard went on to say, "I bought this horse a few months ago for thirty-five thousand dollars. I want to take you guys back to the barn when we get to the track. We can see him and talk to my trainer."

Joe and I did just that. The horse was a beautiful, graceful, black, shiny animal that looked to me like it had the makings of a winner for sure. He was just a great big, marvelous animal that I felt right away could run with the best of them. We talked to the trainer and the trainer said, "Yes. This horse has the willpower and the strength to win races. He's going to win today. I timed him this morning for thirty-six seconds for an eighth of a mile work out. I just know he's ready and he's going to win. I really recommend that you bet on him."

We went up to the club house and had lunch and bet some of the early races. Our minds were really on the seventh race. Howard could do nothing but talk about that horse. He was as nervous as a cat waiting for the seventh race to come up. Then a few minutes before the seventh race was to be run, we went down to the paddock and waited for the trainer to bring the horse up and have it saddled.

We waited a few minutes at the paddock but the horse didn't show. And, all the time, Howard kept wondering where his horse was. If the trainer didn't hurry, the seventh race would be getting under way. Finally, the trainer showed up and it was pretty plain to us something was wrong.

"Mr. Sober," he said. "I've got some bad news for you. When the groom was bringing your horse out of the stable, the horse tripped and broke his front sesamoid." Howard looked at the trainer questioningly for a few moments. Finally, he asked, "What in hell is a sesamoid? Is a broken one serious?"

"It's a bone in a horse's front leg. Your horse has broken his leg, Mr. Sober. I'm sorry about it. The vet at the track has examined the horse and it's his opinion there's nothing can be done for it except to put him humanely away. It's the vet who says the leg is broken."

Howard stared at the trainer in disbelief and could only shake his head. It was hard for him to accept that such a beautiful animal had to be destroyed. I think it was tough for him to do but he said, "Well, if that is what the vet says then you have my authority to do it."

Howard turned to us and said, "Can you believe it? I paid thirty-five thousand dollars for that horse and never ran a race with it. What a terrible disappointment this is."

I looked at Howard in sympathy. That horse was just beautiful, and the thought of it being destroyed was almost too much for me too. I didn't know what to say but a thought ran through my mind that if somebody was willing to take care of it, and see that the leg got healed, that maybe, the horse wouldn't have to be destroyed after all. Of course, it would never be any good for track racing again.

"Howard," I said. "I know you're bitterly disappointed over what happened to this animal, and I am truly sorry about it. But does it have to be destroyed? I own some land up in East Lansing on Park Lake Road where I could keep the horse and try to heal its leg. If I can get him in shape, it would be a wonderful thing to have him there to take care of him, and look after him, and possibly ride him once in a while."

Howard didn't answer me right off but only looked at me. Then, he said, "Okay. But, I don't think a broken leg will heal worth a damn though. Anyway, you're welcome to try. You can have him for a dollar. Just get that horse out of here as quick as you can."

I said, "Howard, you made yourself a deal. Here's the dollar. You give me the papers, and I'll take this horse off your hands right now." The trainer went back and got the papers and Howard signed the horse over to me.

I had to do some fast manipulating on this deal to get the horse out of the track. I didn't really know how to do it. I left the racetrack and ran across the road to a restaurant, where I called the Michigan State University Veterinarian Department. I talked to one of the doctors there and I told him the story, and asked him if they could pick up the horse, take him to East Lansing, look him over, and then give me an opinion if anything could be done for him.

The vet agreed to send a van down for the horse. As a matter of fact, the van was there in less than an hour after I called them. They put the horse in a sling, put him in the van, and took him back to Michigan State University. I watched him go and I gave him a little pat on the rump as they were loading him. "Keep your chin up, old buddy," I said. "If anything can be done to save you, I'll do it. After all, even if you can't race any more, you're still the first race horse I've ever owned."

The next morning, I went over to Michigan State University to the Vet Department and talked to the doctor. I sat down in his office, and he looked at me rather strangely and asked, "Mr. Knowles, who told you that horse had a broken sesamoid?"

I could tell by his tone of voice that he was puzzled over something. "Why," I said, "the vet at the race track examined him and said the only thing to do with the horse was to destroy it."

"Well," he said, "That horse doesn't have a broken sesamoid. I can put that horse in a plastic splint, and I can have him walking in ten days to two weeks, and I can have him galloping in three weeks and running races in five weeks." My mouth about fell open at that news.

"I don't know anybody," he continued, "who would diagnose a thing like that as a broken sesamoid and then have that horse destroyed."

I said, "Well, if I hadn't been there, doctor, that's exactly what would have been done."

He only shook his head. "That certainly would have been a great shame because he is a beautiful animal, and he'll make a good race horse eventually."

I didn't know what to do from there on. I drove over to Joe's house, and found him in his basement recreation room. I said, "Joe. I've got a story that you won't believe." I went on to tell him what had happened. The vet had given me some X-ray prints and had gone over them carefully with me, and I showed them to Joe. He was aghast as well. Neither of us knew what to say.

Finally, Joe spoke. "John. You have to tell Howard about this. It is the damndest thing I have ever heard of. But, you've just got to tell Howard about it."

"Okay," I said. "But we'll do it my way. Make a luncheon appointment with Howard as soon you can but don't tell him what it's all about. Just tell Howard I have something to discuss with him."

Joe made a luncheon appointment with Howard the next day at Jim's restaurant downtown. We sat down at the table and I told Howard the story. He looked at me in disbelief. "I don't believe it," he said. "I don't believe something like that could happen."

I shrugged my shoulders. "It's the truth Howard," I said. "Here's the vet's name and telephone number at Michigan State. Call him and see what he says."

Howard did just that. He walked over to the telephone and he must have talked to that vet for fifteen or twenty minutes. When he came back, he had an incredulous look on his face. "I've never heard of anything like this in my life," he said. "Somebody at the Detroit Race Course is going to pay for this."

He sat down and said, "John, I want to buy my horse back. Under the conditions of this unexpected happening, I think I have the right to buy him back."

I said, "Howard, you're certainly welcome to buy him back. That's one of the reasons I met with you today. That horse is a pretty valuable animal."

"I know you got some expenses involved in this crazy deal," Howard said. "I'll make them all good. The van, the X-ray, the veterinary expenses, the time you spent. I'll make them all good for you." He took his checkbook out of his coat pocket and coolly wrote out a check to me for five thousand dollars and laid it on my plate in front of me. "This should give you some betting money," he said, "and, it should take care of any trouble you went to."

I picked up the check and looked at it carefully. "That's

94

quite a large amount," I said. And, then I tore the check up into small pieces and threw it on the table.

A blank look came on Howard's face when I did that. "You mean five thousand isn't enough to satisfy you?" he asked. "I thought that was a fair offer." I didn't say anything. Howard just sat there and stared at me. Joe was sitting beside me and I could see he felt uncomfortable about this whole thing.

"I can't believe your attitude," Howard said.

He picked up his checkbook again, and wrote out another check for ten thousand dollars and threw it on my plate. "Here," he said. "If that's not enough for you, Knowles, you can keep the horse and I don't care what happens to him." I picked up the check and looked at it just as carefully. Then I tore it up into shreds and threw it on the table.

"I can't believe this," Howard sputtered. "I always thought you were a fair and honest man, Knowles. But, I'm going to tell everybody how you have taken advantage of me on a deal that I really had nothing to do with in the first place. I'm going to have you blackballed from every place I go in Lansing."

I just sat there and let Howard berate me. Then Joe got in the act, "My God, John," he said. "You're both friends of mine. We've had a lot of fun together. You can't do something like this to Howard. I sure would like to see this thing settled. Why don't you two try to come up with something else?"

Howard said, "Okay, I'll try with this guy one more time. Just how much will you take, Knowles, to give me back my horse and my papers?"

I grinned at Howard. I said, "Howard, I want to tell you something. This is the first time you have actually asked me how much you would have to pay to get the horse back. You've beat around the bush for an hour, getting upset, and trying to bribe me with five and ten thousand dollar checks. But, now you have finally come out from behind the bushes and asked me a direct question. And, I will answer it directly. I want you to pay me one dollar which is exactly what I paid for the horse."

Howard kept on sputtering when I said that. "I don't believe you Knowles," he said. "That horse is too damn valuable for you to give him up so easy. And, you've got me where the hair is short. I've signed over the papers to you and there's nothing I can do about it. If you want, you could make a great deal of money racing that horse."

Then he stopped talking and looked directly at me. He knew right then and there I meant what I said because I wasn't arguing with him at all, but just sitting there letting him work me over. He glanced down at the table at all those torn up checks and then looked back up at me. "Well, John," he continued, now he had calmed down. "I guess I was wrong about you. I'm sorry about what I said. I want to apologize—I had you figured all wrong." He wrote out a check for one dollar and gave it to me. We shook hands and I gave Howard back his papers. And, you know, I never cashed that check and I have saved it to this day.

There's a finale to this story. The vet at Michigan State fixed the horse up just like he said he would. Howard took it back to the Detroit Race Course and started winning races with it. He also had the veterinarian at the race track fired. I was sorry about that but that's the way it goes.

Both Howard and Joe died several years ago. I feel a great sense of loss every time I drive by Doc Heckert's old house on Grand River Avenue near Michigan State University. I drive by and see the parking area where these two wonderful guys would be waiting for me. They would be all filled with enthusiasm and grinning with their racing forms tucked under their arms. They couldn't get in the car quick enough to get going to the track.

Now, I never made a lot of money at the race track even
when I owned horses. I made some money but when you stop
and think about it and figure up the expenses, you can see why
they call it the sport of kings. You pay a thousand a month per
horse for training and feeding. If you have two or three or four
of those animals that mounts up pretty fast. Then you have to
add in the shoeing, the veterinary bills, the different special
foods you have to buy. I'll tell you it adds up in a helluva
hurry.

There is one thing about owning a horse. You get a great
thrill when you saddle it up before a race, and then go back to
your table in the clubhouse and sit there watching the race.
Maybe your horse will break from the pack in the stretch, and
come in and win by a nose or a neck or even a couple of
lengths. Then you just stand up and cheer. It's such a great
thrill. There is no question about it. Horse racing is fun. You
can get so wrapped up in it that you can easily go broke.

I guess I will never forget that first racehorse I owned and
the story behind it. There were other horses I owned, but
owning that beautiful racehorse even if it was for a day only,
made me want to buy more and to get even more involved with
the thrill of racing.

14

Life On The Farm
Part One

In 1964, I retired and looked for something to do that would keep me physically in shape and also make a little money. Eventually, I decided to take up Christmas tree farming. So, I leased a rundown, neglected tree farm in East Lansing, Michigan.

I went into it with an open mind. I really didn't know anything about trees, but I thought it would be a wonderful thing to plant them, take care of them, and be out of doors and next to nature. I studied all I could about trees and I took classes at Michigan State University to learn more. The one thing I wasn't aware of when I started the business is that people were forever stealing Christmas trees. They would come in at all times of the day and night and either cut them down themselves or steal those that had already been cut.

As I said, the place had been neglected and rundown. The trees hadn't been trimmed for years and they were covered with every kind of insect you could think of including saw flies. But, by hard work and study, I made that farm into a beautiful piece of wild land. It was about four hundred acres of trees and ponds, and it was the last piece of decent forest land anywhere in the county.

After I got that farm into production and got it squared away, I would ship trees to buyers in Florida, California, Texas and to practically anywhere in the United States. And, if you can believe it, those trees would sell for about seventy-five cents each wholesale back then when I first started.

I had so many trees stolen over the years. People would come in and cut two or three trees, drag them out to the road, throw them in their car, and drive away as though those trees were just growing wild on the property. Others would come in and steal on a much larger scale.

I remember one year, I had a bunch of trees lined up for shipping. They were all baled, tied up with string, counted and stacked in a field right by my house. I went out one morning and discovered that a whole bunch of those trees had been taken. I could see the tracks where whoever had did it had pulled trees from the pile, and dragged them to their truck or car and driven off with them.

"By God," I said to myself, "Enough's enough." Money was short for me in those days and the loss of a few trees meant a great deal to me. I didn't know exactly what to do to stop it but I had an idea.

That night, I took a loaded shotgun and walked out and hid myself in those trees in the dark, and waited to see if anyone else was going to come along and help themselves. My wife was upset when she saw the loaded gun. "Be careful," she said. "Those thieves might have guns too and then what will you do?"

I said. "We'll find out one way or the other."

It was a chilly moonlit night but I went back in the first bunch of trees I had stacked and sat down. I lighted my pipe and put my shotgun between my knees and just waited.

Sure enough, here comes a truck along the road with its lights off. Pretty soon it stops right alongside my pile of trees, and two guys jump out and start running trees one at a time and throwing them on the truck. They did this right in front of me and never saw me at all. I let them put about twenty trees on the truck, and then I walked out from behind the stack, pointed the shotgun at them and shouted, "Put your hands in the air."

Well, you never saw any more two surprised individuals in your life. But, they did exactly what I told them. I marched them up to my house. On the way, I kept threatening them with what I would do if they tried anything. I guess I was as scared as they were but I didn't dare let on. Anyway, I told them I would blow their heads off if they even made one sudden move. "You bastards," I said. "Coming in here and stealing my Christmas trees."

When I got to the house, I made them lie face down in the snow. Then I kicked on the door with my foot to call my wife. Never once did I relax my hold on that shotgun or point it anywhere but in their direction. My wife Marge came to the door and took one look at those guys lying there on the ground and me with the shotgun. "Oh my God," she gasped, "You've killed them. I knew it! I knew it!"

"No," I said. Her reaction was funny enough to make me laugh. "Call the sheriff will you?" The sheriff came right away and arrested these guys—took them in and took their truck. I had to go to St. Johns, the county seat, two days later to appear in court. I had the satisfaction of seeing these guys sent to jail but I never did get paid for any of those trees they stole.

Shipping Christmas Trees

That was the way it went in the Christmas tree business; it was a losing game most of the time. Even worse than tree thieves were the crooked operators—the wholesaler who bought the trees from the grower. These crooked operators were more numerous than you could imagine, and some of them were pretty slick in their dealings.

Once I had a guy from West Virginia call me two weeks before Christmas looking for a thousand trees. He told me over the phone that he ran a big company called the Riverside Lumber Company and he needed these trees right away. It just so happened that I had a thousand cut trees that I hadn't sold and were ready to be shipped.

I said, "Yes. I've got a thousand trees but I have to have the money up front before I'll sell them to you."

"I haven't got time to send you the money, Mr. Knowles," he said. "But, I give you my word if you send those trees down to me, I will pay your truck driver in cash on the spot when he gets here."

I knew if I didn't sell those trees right away, they wouldn't be sold at all. So I decided to take the gamble. I shipped the trees to him that day and told my driver. "Under no circumstances are you to unload one single tree until you get paid in cash."

In a few days the driver was back and I was waiting for him. He waved an envelope at me from the truck window. "Here's your money," he said. "That guy paid me just like he said."

I opened the envelope. That son of a gun had cut newspapers to the size of dollar bills and filled that envelope with those newspaper clippings. On top of that, he had written a check for the amount of three thousand dollars for the trees. But, it was written on one of those checks that you buy in packages at Woolworth's with no bank name on them. You fill them out like a receipt book, except it's for checks. I looked at that check and he had written the name of some bank in West Virginia on it. I suspected right then I had been had.

Anyway, I took the check to my banker and asked him what he thought about it. He took one look at it and said, "This thing looks phony as anything to me. But, I'll check out the bank name for you and call you back tomorrow."

The next morning he called and said, "John. There is no such bank in West Virginia."

I asked him, "What's my recourse?"

"Not much," he said. "You can't collect on this check. It's obvious the guy has given you a bad one. I guess you could go down there and sue him but how much is your time and trouble worth? You would have to do it all down in West Virginia."

I thought about that for a while. Three thousand dollars was a lot of money to me that year. I was mad and upset. I decided right then that he was not going to get away with it. I knew just what I was going to do about it. I called the airport and got a round trip ticket to Charleston, West Virginia and made reservations for going down and coming back on the same day. I told Marge I would be back that night. I was going down to West Virginia to collect my money. But before I left, I packed a .38 Smith and Wesson revolver in my back pocket.

When the airplane got to Charleston, I took a taxi cab to the prosecuting attorney's office. I went in and introduced myself and said, "I'm John Knowles from East Lansing, Michigan. I'm a Christmas tree farmer and I'm having some troubles with one of your guys down here and I wonder if you can help me out?"

"All depends," he said. "What's his name?"

"He's the fellow that runs The Riverside Lumber Company," I said.

He pushed his chair back from his desk and went over to his files. Pretty soon he came back with a large folder. "Mr. Knowles," he said. "You'll have to get in line because there's about forty-eight complaints ahead of you about Christmas trees with this guy."

"Is there anything I can do?" I asked.

"Well, you can do what some of these other guys have done. You can start a suit against him and if they give you a judgment, you can try to collect. I know the guy hasn't got anything. We've been looking to put him in jail, but we haven't been able to find enough evidence of fraud to be able to arrest him."

"What about this bad check that he wrote me? Is that

enough to bring him to court?"

"Well, I think I can have him arrested on that."

I thought that over for a minute and then said, "I guess I would like to talk to this guy first and see what I can do with him."

He said, "Okay, go ahead. But come back here and report to me before you leave because I want that check. I'll have him arrested if you'll sign a complaint."

I got in a cab and went to the Riverside Lumber Company. I told the driver to wait. The Riverside Lumber Company was a group of Quonset huts with guys running in and out of doors like mad. There were Christmas trees stacked all over the place in piles as high as the roofs of the Quonset huts. I picked out the biggest Quonset hut and went in. There was a guy at the front door and I asked him if I could see "so and so."

"Yeah. I guess you can," he said. "He's sitting at that desk way in the back."

I walked back there and I stood in front of this big fat guy. He didn't pay any attention to me for the longest time. He kept on ignoring me, and after a while he looked up and said, "Okay fella. What can I do for you?"

I said, "Are you Mr. So and So?"

"You got 'im," he said.

"I'm John Knowles from East Lansing," I said. "And I came here to collect some money from you." I reached in my back pocket and pulled out the .38 revolver. I cocked the hammer and put the gun to his head.

I said, "If I don't get my money in two minutes, I'm going to blow your brains all over this desk."

He sat back in his chair and the sweat started to run off him. He was pretty frightened because I could see his eyeballs roll around in his head. "My God, man," he said. "You're crazy. Put that gun away."

"No way buddy," I said. "You're not going to give me the hosing that you gave to those other forty guys. I talked to the prosecuting attorney and I know all about you. That bum check you wrote is enough to send you to jail. I either get my money now or you'll never see Christmas."

He reached down and pulled open the bottom drawer of his desk, a big double drawer. It was packed full of money. I could see hundred-, fifty-, and twenty-dollar bills. He grabbed a wad of bills and counted out thirty-three hundred dollars which was three hundred more than he owed me. I put the money in my coat packet and put the gun away. "You're a lucky guy," I said. "Because if you hadn't had that money in there, you would have been dead just as sure as hell."

I took a long look at him and I could see he was so frightened, he couldn't talk. "Thank you," I said. "It was great doing business with you. Have a Merry Christmas." I turned and walked out the door. I jumped in the cab and went back to the prosecuting attorney's office.

"Well," he said. "Did you find the guy?"

"Oh sure," I said. "But, I'm sorry I won't be able to sign that complaint for you. The guy paid me in full."

The prosecuting attorney looked at me doubtfully and said, "I don't believe it."

I pulled out this wad of dough and took a hundred dollar bill out of it. I stuck it in his coat pocket where he carried his handkerchief. "I'm sure you've got a family and I would like your kids to have a nice Christmas present."

He shook his head. "I'm sorry Mr. Knowles, I can't take that money. I'm a public servant."

I said, "Well, your kids aren't public servants so you give this to them and you'll have a clear conscience."

He stared at me for a long time with a puzzled look on his face. He said, "I can't believe that man would pay you off with all the other people that are lined up here trying to get money." He leaned forward and looked me right in the eye. "Mr. Knowles," he asked, "have you got a gun on you?"

I said, "Well, now why would a man like me carry a gun?"

He pursed his lips together and nodded his head. "Yeah," he said. "Why would a man like you carry a gun? I'm going to tell you something. You have exactly fifteen minutes to get the hell of my office and my county and get to the airport, and get on an airplane and go back to Lansing. I never want to see you down here again." Then he said, "Just how in hell did you get that money?"

I said, "The less you know about it, the happier we'll all be."

I took off out of there and caught my airplane and came back home. Marge was waiting for me when I got back. It was 9:30 at night when I walked into the house. "Did you collect the money?" she asked.

I said, "Oh yes, dear. Here it is."

She said, "Did you have any trouble?"

I said, "No."

She said, "I can't understand why that man didn't pay you in the first place without you going down there to collect."

I said, "Well, it's a long story, dear. I'll tell you all about it sometime." I went to bed.

15

Life On The Farm
Part Two

You might think that raising Christmas trees was a matter of planting the trees, letting them grow for a few years, and then harvesting them. After all, whoever planted a forest or a woods? They were just there and the trees grew and took care of themselves the way nature intended it. In the Christmas tree business, it didn't work that way. There were bugs and thieves, and other problems you can't imagine. It was very hard work; sometimes the solution to one problem only meant the creation of more problems.

I joined a Christmas tree association in order to find out what others were doing to improve their business. One day, at one of the meetings, some guy talked about the trouble with keeping the lanes between the Christmas trees mowed, how much it cost and how much labor, time and machinery were involved. Another fellow stood up and said, "Well, I have found the answer to all that labor. I bought some sheep, turned them loose, and they keep those lanes mowed better than I can mow them with a machine."

I had a lot of lanes that I mowed on my farm, and I spent plenty of time and money doing it. So I was open to any good idea. I listened to this guy very carefully, and when I got back home, I called a couple of friends of mine and asked them if they had any sheep for sale.

One friend said, "Yes, I have some. I'll sell you all you want."

I said, "Bring me twenty-five." That sounded like a nice even number of sheep to start with.

The next morning, I fenced in a neat little area where I wanted the sheep to roam. I had visions of sheep grazing away contentedly on my farm and getting fat. Maybe I could even market a few and have a mutton dinner now and then when the herd got too big. Above all, I would have trim grassy areas between my rows of trees that would keep the bugs down, and allow my trees to get plenty of nourishment.

That afternoon, the guy showed up with a truckload of sheep. Amid all the baa-baas and pushing and shoving, we got them unloaded. They went right away to feeding. Once they felt at home, they were well behaved and seemed very happy. The lanes between the Christmas trees were grassy and green and the sheep really went for them. I stood and watched for a while and felt that these sheep were the perfect answer to my grass problem.

The next morning, I went out to check on them, and I had to stop and take a second look at what I saw. The ground between the Christmas trees in the pen was absolutely bare. There wasn't even a hint that there had been grass there before. It was bare right down to the soil. There wasn't anything else to do but build a larger pen. So I tore down the old fence and made a bigger range for them to roam in. In a few days, that was cropped right down to the earth.

I kept on doing that; every two or three days, I would go out and the sheep would have the ground between the Christmas trees cropped bare. I would build new fences and tear down the old fences and move the sheep to a new area. It was a continual, never-ending job of extending the pasture. I had one helluva time with it. I began to think that the time spent mowing the grass with machinery wasn't that much wasted time after all.

Then the neighborhood dogs got into the act. There were a lot of stray dogs around the country, and it didn't take them long to find the sheep. The dogs would sneak into the pen at night and run those sheep ragged and even kill some of them.

My wife and I would be sleeping, and she would wake up in the middle of the night, hear those dogs barking and say, "John, wake up, the dogs are after the sheep again."

I would jump up and get dressed, take my shotgun and go down there to shoot at the damn dogs. That went on, night after night, driving me crazy. I spent all day building new pastures, and all night protecting the sheep from dogs. This went on for weeks and weeks, and I was really getting worn out.

While I was dealing with those situations, I found another terrible, shocking problem I had to deal with in raising sheep. It came as a complete surprise to me; I wasn't even aware that sheep could have such a problem. One morning, as I was getting ready to move another section of fence, I saw one sheep lying down, and it looked like it was dead. I went over to it and tried to get it to move but it just lay there pathetically looking up at me. I rolled it over to see if it had been hurt, and I was just staggered at what I saw. There was a great big ball of writhing, ugly maggots on its rear end that were practically eating it alive.

"My God, I thought, What is happening here?" I was so disturbed and upset that I went and called the friend who sold me the sheep.

He laughed and said, "John, this is a normal thing for sheep and we can take care of the problem. Sheepherders deal with it all the time. I'll be down to give you a hand."

He showed up the next day with what he called "sheep dip" on his truck. We set this thing up and then set up a corral. We would get the sheep in the corral, and then run them through the sheep dip tanks. It was dirty, stinky, smelly work and it took us a week and a half to finish the job. But, it did cure whatever it was these sheep had. By the time we were through, I had had enough of sheep raising. I told my friend, "look, I bought these animals and I paid you for them. But, I am going to give them back to you. I don't want any money for them—not even a dime. I have had all the experience as a sheepherder that I will ever want in my life."

He laughed and said, "Okay, if you want to give these sheep back. I'll take them."

We loaded everything on his truck: the sheep dip, the corrals, the pens, and all the other stuff he brought down with him. He had two guys working with him, and it was a helluva job. He took all that away, then came back with the truck, and we corralled the sheep and put them in the truck and he took off.

I watched him going down the road and I heard the sheep baaing as he disappeared from sight. "Good-bye, you sonuva-guns!" I shouted at them and shook my fist. "I don't ever want to see another sheep on my property again!"

After that, I was content to hear the sound of a tractor-drawn power mower whining away as it chopped down the offending grass between my trees. At times, I could almost believe that the sound blended pretty well with the other sounds of nature in my little natural world of Christmas trees.

16

My Log Cabin
In The Woods

My Christmas tree farm took long hours of hard work. Still, one thing that came out of it brought me gratification. I had always wanted to build a log cabin of my own in the woods. On the farm I had a large stand of Norway pine that had grown to twenty or thirty feet high. They were straight and healthy, and I guess in the back of my mind, I was saving them for the day I could use them to build the log cabin I had always dreamed about.

One day a neighbor of mine came to me and asked about those trees. I told him they never sold very well as Christmas trees because I specialized in premium Douglas firs.

"They would be just the thing to build a log cabin with," he said. He never looked directly at me when he said it and I suspected he was angling for a favor.

"Yes," I replied, and waited for him to continue.

"I've got this piece of property a couple of miles from here on the Looking Glass River that would be just right for a log cabin. But the labor and cost of materials might be a little too much for me to handle right now," he said. "It's a pretty little spot among the trees and the cabin would make a nice summer home. Why don't you come over and take a look at the property?"

I did just that and fell in love with the place. I could see in my mind's eye exactly how it would look and what had to be done.

"I'm glad you agree, John" he said. "Those Norway pines of yours would fit the bill, wouldn't they? Now admit it, you're never going to sell them. How about letting me use them to build this log cabin? I could pay you when times are a little better for me. My handyman Rick will do the building but we could always use your advice on building it. I know building a log cabin is a dream of yours, and this will help you make that dream come true."

I liked the idea and told him so. I love to work with my hands and the thought of helping build a log cabin sounded good to me.

"Great," he said. "Rick'll be over to help you cut the trees tomorrow."

I was so enthused, I went out and bought a book on how to build a log cabin and read it from cover to cover. Rick proved to be a very cheerful, hard working young man, and he and I got along very well. But the neighbor never lifted a hand. Instead, he kept asking me questions on how I would do so and so or this and that, and how hard it would be for Rick to handle those logs by himself.

"Don't you think it should be done this way, John?" he would ask. "How would you do it?" So when it came time to build the cabin, I found myself working right along with Rick to make sure everything was done right.

"John," the neighbor would say. "I don't know how I'll ever repay you? But, I will. I will."

Rick and I decided to make the cabin twenty-five by twenty-five. It was going to be straight and square. We cut some terrific logs, hauled them out to his property, put them on saw horses, and used draw knives to skin the bark back. Rick and I worked on the cabin every day during the entire winter and it was hard, tough work. The logs were big and heavy to handle; they all had to be carefully notched and put together. When we got the cabin up in place, we drove hemp rope in between the logs to make it weather proof. We put in an absolutely beautiful pine floor, sanded it, and used a clear varnish so that it had a natural finish.

We built the cabin right next to the Looking Glass River, and built a porch all around the cabin so you could sit on the front porch and drop a fishing line right in the river. Through the trees in the evening, you could see the sun set, and be completely surrounded by natural beauty that was the equal of anything on a river in northern Michigan. I am sure that if the cabin had been built up there, it would have been worth thousands of dollars.

While we were building it, the neighbor would come out and admire it and tell us what a wonderful job we were doing. One day, Rick said to him, "This is sure going to be beautiful, boss. When the tax assessor sees it, he's gonna assess you top dollar."

"Oh," the neighbor said. "I don't worry about that. They don't know a thing about this place. I didn't get a building permit. If anybody says anything, I'll just tell them it was on the property when I bought it."

Both Rick and I looked at each other in amazement. That

confirmed the suspicions I had been having about this neighbor. I began to realize that he had no intention of paying me for the work I was doing. He always spoke about how much he owed me but his pockets were too deep for him to find any money in them. It was always a promise of things to come. But, by the time that was clear to me, the work was finished.

He never did pay me—not even for the logs. Never once did I get to stay in it. His promises were always for future payments when times got better for him. I realize I was a fish for being taken in, but at the time, building such a cabin had always been my dream.

Despite what he did to me, I will always have the quiet satisfaction of knowing that I created something beautiful and worthwhile that I had always dreamed about. And, I think the pleasure I get from knowing that is worth far more than any money he might have paid me.

17

Butch Schram

I have had many wonderful hunting and fishing guides in my life: Joe Case, Freddie Green, and Napoleon Vincent, to name a few. All of them were remarkable in their own way and made my hunting and fishing adventures much more enjoyable. But the guide that stands out in my memory as being the most remarkable was a fellow by the name of Butch Schram. He was quite a guy. His lifestyle was entirely his own and he lived the way he wanted to. Butch had many talents, including the carving of wooden duck decoys. His decoys were works of art. I do a little carving myself, so I have a good many books and magazines on making decoys. One of those books features decoys by all the noted carvers in the world, and Butch Schram is mentioned in that book.

I first met Butch sometime in the 1950's when Fred Glass and I went to Lake St. Clair to a place called Fair Haven to fly fish for small mouth bass. Butch had a small boat livery there and we rented a boat from him. We got to talking, and he was such an interesting person, and so enthusiastic about duck hunting, that both Fred and I decided to come back in the fall and do some hunting with him.

Butch lived on an island in Lake St. Clair; the only way to reach him was by boat. You had to let him know when you were coming so that he could meet you at the dock and pick you up. He lived there with his beautiful Indian wife and they were the most compatible couple I have ever seen. Butch trapped for muskrats and I have seen him and his wife work side by side, skinning and scraping hides or carving decoys. It reminded me so much of the way Indian families in the early days must have shared their lives with each other—each doing what they could do best and working to support the other.

Butch Schram

I can remember going to Butch's house in the fall after the trapping season. He would have wires strung a foot or so apart from one side of a room to the other. On these wires, he would have thousands of muskrat hides hanging on stretchers. The place smelled pretty bad and you had to take a deep breath and hold it before you went in. He sold those hides and their sale constituted a good portion of his income; he also sold muskrat meat. There was a restaurant way down on the east side of Detroit that would buy it, because a lot of people considered muskrat a delicacy. As a matter of fact, I once had some neighbors that just loved the taste of muskrat. They told me it was the most wonderful meat. But after smelling all those muskrat hides in Butch's house, I don't know whether I could ever eat any of the meat.

To help Butch out, one year I brought a friend of mine, who was a fur buyer at Wall Lake. The friend, Harry, had asked me if I knew anybody that had any muskrat hides. I told him about Butch and he said, "Well, let's go out there and I'll buy all the rats he's got."

I drove Harry down to Lake St. Clair and we met Butch at the dock. At the time, I think Butch had about four thousand muskrat hides. He wanted $4.25 apiece for them.

My friend checked over the hides, and saw that Butch and his wife had done an excellent job of skinning and stretching, and that the fur was prime quality. He sat right down at the table in Butch's house and wrote out a check for about sixteen thousand dollars.

Butch watched him for a minute and then said, "Mister, I don't know you from the next tourist that walks down the dock at Fair Haven, and I don't know how much money you've got in the bank. Your check could stretch all the way from here to the mainland for all I know. Four thousand hides is a helluva lot of time and labor for me and I just won't take your check."

Harry looked at me in surprise. I could see he was upset. "Well, John, will you tell me just how in the hell this guy thinks I'm going to pay for all those muskrat hides? I don't carry that much cash on me."

Butch said, "Well, I know John. I'll take his check. You can write your check out to John."

I laughed at that. Harry had a million dollars in the bank, and I think I had thirty dollars in my checking account that particular day. And Butch was asking *me* to write a check for sixteen thousand dollars for a bunch of muskrat hides. I turned to Harry and said, "Hey, if I write this check, I gotta be damn sure I get your money tomorrow, right?"

Harry said, "Okay John. I don't see any problem with that." So I sat down and wrote Butch a check.

But, that was Butch—just as independent as the island he lived on. Maybe that was one of the things I liked about him, and why I would stick my neck out for him and write a check out for a lot of money I didn't have.

Fred and I did a lot of duck hunting with Butch in Saginaw Bay. He was the best guide for that sport; he had his own unique way of doing it. He owned a big cruiser for going out on the bay and a sneak boat that he carried along to hunt the ducks from. We would go out on Saginaw Bay at about four o'clock in the morning. Butch would put out a couple of hundred decoys in various places. Then he would go upwind and anchor maybe a quarter or a half mile away. We would sit out of the weather in his cruiser, drinking coffee and waiting for Butch to call the ducks in.

The first morning we went out with Butch there were clouds of ducks getting up all around us in the dark and they sounded like freight trains in motion. There seemed to be millions of them out there. There was almost no effort to getting your limit which I think was six in those days. It was quite a fun way to hunt.

When a bunch of ducks would come over, Butch would call them and they would swing around and land at the decoys. One of us would get in the front of the sneak boat, and Butch would pole us over downwind until we got within shooting range of the ducks.

The sneak boat had a collapsible blind like a windshield in the front with a couple of peep holes in it. We would crouch down behind that and then jump up and shout. The ducks would take off in a flurry and we would try to hit one or two of them. That was real fun shooting.

The other guy would be back in the cruiser watching with a pair of binoculars. If we missed a shot, we heard about it when we got back. The jokes and horse laughs would come down pretty heavy but it was all good fun. It made us make damn sure that when we pulled that trigger, we hit the ducks, rather than just scattering a bunch of shot at the rising birds.

Butch had a way of calling those ducks that was all his own. When we would see a big string of ducks off on the horizon, Butch would cup his hands and call them with his mouth. It wasn't a manufactured call; he called them naturally with his voice. Those ducks—I saw it happen so many times—were like they were on a string. They would turn almost at the first call and come over and land by those decoys. It was amazing the way Butch could call ducks. That was the secret of his success in guiding for duck hunting. And it gave the hunters he guided so many opportunities to get their limit.

Through the years, Freddie and I went down there both to hunt and fish and we became very good friends of Butch. I often wish I had gotten some of those duck decoys from him.

He must have had four or five hundred, all carved by him and his wife. They were works of art and collector's items.

Butch was unique in his own way. I guess it is fitting that Butch is remembered by all his beautiful decoys. The times I spent hunting and fishing with Butch are full of memories of a remarkable individual, and a wonderful and outstanding guide. They still stay with me after all these years.

18

Canada O' Canada
Part 1

For a number of years after my retirement, I operated a fishing and hunting lodge in Canada in the Ranger Lake area north of Saulte Ste Marie, Canada. It was a beautiful part of the Ontario wilderness and the Canadian shield country, filled with gorgeous little lakes teeming with walleye and pike, and cold running streams chuck full of speckled trout. There was all kinds of wildlife right at the front door of the lodge—beaver, mink, otter, moose, loons, ducks and eagles. It was an idyllic spot because it was wild, primitive country and I loved being there.

The lodge was located on Ranger Lake and had a boat house right on the lake. I had nine cabins with inside plumbing and electricity. There were two generators in a generator house about two hundred yards away from the lodge; one was an emergency generator, and one we operated all day long. All the cabins were completely furnished—you could go there and spend a week or two, and live like a king right in the middle of the Canadian wilderness.

I had a complete staff up there—a cook and an assistant cook, and four or five girls to wait on tables, make the beds, clean up and do the housework. Also, there were three or four young men to take care of the boats and motors. They equipped the boats and rented them to our guests. A boat and motor was the first thing most guests asked for when they arrived so they could go fishing. There was an ice house which I kept stocked with ice. Every year right after Christmas, guys from the local ranger station would go out on the lake, cut ice, and fill the ice house. We had ice all summer long, and anybody that wanted to take fresh fish home had no problem going out to the ice house and getting all they needed.

One of the delightful little things I remember about that lodge was an old wooden backhouse located about a hundred yards behind the main building. It had a half moon cut in the door and was only a two holer. I was tempted to take the thing down several times when I took over the lodge, but it was so unique and funny that I left it.

There was a little stream that ran down from Samo Lake over an old lumber dam, and then through my property and into Ranger Lake. It was about a half mile long—just a pretty little stream that rambled its way through the trees and the rocks and right past the front of that little old backhouse.

I went out and cleaned up that outdoor toilet; I scrubbed it all down and got rid of the insects and other debris, and found that whoever built it had done a pretty good job. The best part was that the door opened up facing this little stream that came tumbling down from Samo Lake. How I loved to go out there in the morning, and sit and watch that little stream, and contemplate the beauty of nature that was all around me. It was one of the most picturesque places imaginable; especially early in the coming up.

I sold my lodge later on, and I often wonder if the new owners kept that old backhouse, and if they found the serenity and charm that I found in it.

Mother Nature in Canada had ways of keeping us in line so that we didn't get too carried away with the scenery. One of her particular little charms was the black flies. They only came early in the spring and when they did they were unbearable.

You never felt the bite of a black fly, and you never knew when you were bitten until blood streamed down your face or your hands or wherever they bit you. They just loved to get under your clothes and have a feast on your more sensitive parts around your ankles or waist. The itch from them drives you mad.

I remember one year, I took my wife Marge up early in the spring to show her the lodge. The black flies were terrible; they came in swarms and attacked any living thing they could find. Every time she went outdoors they swarmed around her. She was allergic to their bite and had to stay indoors the whole week. After that, she never would go up to the lodge in the spring or at any time she thought that the black flies might be out.

I had one guest who came to me at noon one day and asked, "My God, Mr. Knowles, what can I do? I can't fish. I can't go outside. Those black flies are driving me crazy." He pulled up his pants, and rolled down his socks, and his ankles were so bitten up by black flies that they looked like a piece of beef steak.

I took him inside and doctored him as best I could. I told him, "Tie your pant legs down with a piece of twine or shoestring so that the black flies can't get down inside your pants like that."

The black flies were really something else in the spring. I would take packages and boxes of Amoco Number Fifteen repellent with me. I kept it stocked regularly at the lodge. It was the best thing I could find to cope with those pests. In season, we used up a can or two of the stuff every day. The black flies seemed to come at certain times, and at other times we would be comparatively free. I know there were a lot of times when I didn't have any flies to contend with at all. I never could figure that out.

The Indians that lived by the lodge had their own way of dealing with the black flies. You would see them walking around carrying a branch in their hand to use as a fly swatter to brush the black flies away from their faces. They would swing it back and forth around their faces all the time.

Mother Nature was always at her wild best with the back roads up in Canada. The lodge was about seventy miles from Saulte Ste Marie, and about forty-five miles of that was gravel road. It was the worst gravel road I have ever driven on; it was like a tank trap. There were so many holes and rocks in the road that it could tear the bottom of your car up in an instant.

Many of our guests had holes punched in their gas tanks by those roads, and then were stranded in the middle of nowhere in that wilderness. Usually there would be no traffic for days at a time. You just had a helluva time if you didn't have an extra tank of gas with you for an emergency, because you might sit there for two or three days waiting for someone to come along.

One guest named Don from Bloomfield Hills, Michigan was leaving to go home and I had to go to the Soo to get some parts for my generators. I told him I would follow him out. It was lucky I did because halfway down that gravel road, he punched a hole in his gas tank and lost all his gas. There he was sitting by the side of the road when I came along.

There was an Indian woman who owned a piece of property and a house on that road. I had made friends with her and had stopped at her house several times to admire the malamutes that she raised. She raced them all over the country in sled dog races. She was a widow; her husband had been killed in a hunting accident, and she lived there by herself. She hunted and trapped and chopped all her wood and was completely self-sufficient.

I pulled Don's car into her front yard, and she came out to see what was the matter. She nodded her head and laughed when we told her. Then she went back behind her house, and got a double-bitted axe, and made a couple of hemlock plugs. She took a look at the holes, trimmed those hemlock plugs to size and pounded them into the gas tank. "Just like new," she said. "That'll keep you till you get to the Soo."

I followed Don all the way to Saulte Ste Marie and he didn't have a bit of trouble. Afterwards, he told me he had driven all the way back to Bloomfield Hills with those two hemlock plugs in his gas tank.

In Canada that far north, sometimes as late as the middle of May, there would be snow on those gravel roads, making them impassable. I would go up and open the lodge about the twelfth of May every year. Sometimes, I had a helluva time getting through because of the snow. But despite gravel roads, snow drifts, black flies and everything else, there would usually be people waiting for me to open the lodge. When I would drive in, they would be sitting at the dock waiting for me to show up.

I had all kinds of equipment at my lodge to keep things in shape and for getting around. I had a launch, a Jeep, and a bulldozer. I remember one thing that happened to me with the Jeep; it was rather embarrassing and cost me a lot of money.

The generator building was two hundred yards away from

the main lodge so the noise of the motors wouldn't disturb the guests. It was on the edge of a hill that ran down to Ranger Lake. One morning, I stopped at the generator building to check on something. I left the Jeep with the motor running at the top of the hill. While I was in the building, the Jeep rolled down the hill into the lake and went completely out of sight. When I came back out, the Jeep was nowhere to be seen. You can imagine how perplexed I was to have something like that disappear in a few seconds, especially back there in that wilderness. I had a time figuring out just what had happened.

When I finally realized the Jeep had rolled into the lake, I tried to get it out by myself but had to give up. I got one of the guides to put his bathing suit on and go out and locate it. The water was pretty cold at the time. I think it was just after the ice had gone out. The guide got a chain on the Jeep, and I hooked it to the bulldozer and we pulled it out.

I was pretty embarrassed but my chagrin was nothing compared to what water had done to the engine of that Jeep. I couldn't get it started, and I had to pull the heads off the motor and practically rebuild it. It took a long time to fix that engine. All because I had carelessly parked the Jeep on top of a hill pointed towards the lake without putting the brakes on. You learn something new every day, don't you? We worked on that Jeep motor for two weeks before we could get it to run again.

It was a long trip from my home in Michigan to that lodge in Canada, and I made it every two weeks. But it had to be done because there was always something that needed fixing and taken care of. People looked forward to seeing me there. The rough roads and the long drive took a toll on both me and the car. Then too, sometimes the unusual would happen which would make me wonder whether I shouldn't give it up.

One day, I was on my way back from the lodge to Lansing.

I finally got off the rocky road and onto the paved highway north of the Mackinac Bridge. I was cruising along about seventy miles an hour, and anticipating a nice easy trip the rest of the way. I pulled up to the toll booth on the St. Ignace side, paid my fare, and then started through the gates onto the bridge when smoke started to roll out of the back of my car. I stopped right there on the bridge. I opened the back door to see what was going on. The back of that car practically exploded in flames. All I could do was save some of my luggage. As it was, I got burned in several places doing it.

The bridge authorities called the fire department from St. Ignace. They came out, but what an inept bunch of fire fighters they were. Their hoses were full of leaks, and instead of using the nozzles to squirt water on the fire, they were using the spray from the leaks. It was the damnedest thing. There was my car burning up like a torch, and they were piddling little streams of water on it. God, I wouldn't want to have had a house on fire and have them try to put the fire out.

The car burned up completely. I had the bridge traffic tied up for an hour and a half. People were scrambling around taking pictures and everything else. All I could do was stand there and watch my car burn. I sold what was left of the car to a guy for twenty-five dollars. He had an automobile junkyard in the town right at the bridge entrance.

That was one of the things about going up to the lodge every two or three weeks. It took a lot of driving and a lot of time, and it was really hard on my car. When you got past the bridge, you were going to run into some roads in Canada that were pretty rough. It took a lot of my time and it spread me pretty thin. With all that to put up with and my wife's reluctance to be there with the black flies, I finally gave up and sold the lodge.

I really didn't make much money on it. It was more of a fun project than anything else. But, I have regretted letting go of it in one way, because it was real wild, primitive country with all kinds of wildlife and fishing, and I loved that very much.

19

Canada O' Canada
Part 2

Although I gave up my lodge in the Canadian wilderness, I still have many fond memories of fishing and hunting there. It was my delight to invite my friends up there, and share with them some of my secret fishing spots and the wonderful treats nature provided in the Canadian shield country.

I located two or three lakes with little streams running into them, where you could just catch fish after fish without much effort at all. They were a fisherman's paradise. I found them by just portaging my canoe from lake to lake and following different rivers and streams. It was like exploring a new country and finding one new delight after another.

One particular year, the fishing was especially good for speckled trout and lake trout, and I invited a group of fourteen people from Scientific Anglers to come up and spend a week as my guests. They accepted my invitation, and were a very proficient group of anglers and fly fishermen. They knew how to use tackle and fly rods. I took them to all the different streams and lakes around there where I knew they would catch fish and they had a wonderful time.

The sales manager of the company was so pleased that he gave me a couple of fly rods and reels and a half dozen lines. I still have that equipment. One of those rods I used just this year to go steelheading; it is a beautiful rod, and I am very grateful for it. It brings back many memories of that Canadian lodge.

There is one trip in particular that I remember. It was one of the most enjoyable canoe trips that I took in the Canadian back country.

It started when one of my guests said that he wanted to go on an extraordinary trip. He was a camera buff, and he wanted something different he could talk about. I said, "Well, I know some little lakes and streams we can explore. I'm sure we'll find all kinds of wildlife where you might get some pictures. Be here early tomorrow morning—bring your fishing gear along with your camera."

We started out about five thirty the next morning. We had fifteen miles of lake to travel by canoe, and we just decided to take our time and have a really nice day of it. The lake was calm and as smooth as glass with a morning mist rising on it. As we paddled up the lake, there were loons calling all around us. After spending so much time around the lodge I could imitate a loon call quite well. And they would answer me. So I started calling to them the whole way up the lake. I carried on a conversation with them. It was just wonderful gliding quietly along in that canoe and hearing those loons answer me from all around the lake.

We were also accompanied by otters most of the way up the lake. They would swim alongside the canoe, and then dip under the water and come up on the other side. Sometimes, they would just play around, and other times, they would come over to the canoe and look us over curiously.

As we were going up the lake, I noticed a dark spot on the far side of the lake. I called to my guest in the front of the canoe, "Do you see that black spot over there on the shore on the far side of the lake?"

He said, "Yes, what is it?"

I said, "That's a bear. If you want a picture of it, I'll paddle us over there. You just sit still and don't use your paddle at all."

I slipped my paddle in the water and by twisting it Indian style and not lifting it out of the water, I was able to steer the canoe over towards the bear without making any noise.

It was out of our way but we got across the lake without the bear seeing us, and we got to within maybe five or ten feet of him. The bear never noticed us until my guest started taking pictures of him. I can understand why the bear was not spooked because he would never be expecting danger out on the lake. If any danger came, or anything happened that would frighten him, it would always come from behind him on the land rather than the lake.

As soon as the bear heard the shutter click, he turned around in surprise. He stood up on his legs dumbfounded and aston-ished, wondering where we came from. Then he dropped down onto all fours, and ran off helter-skelter into the bush. We had a good laugh over that.

We continued on down the lake and made a portage to a much smaller lake. Then we came to another portage that would take us to a third lake which I knew was full of speckled trout. It was about a two and a half mile portage and we followed an old game trail to get there. We would take turns carrying the canoe. One of us would carry the duffel and the tackle and then trade off and take the canoe. It took us quite a while to make that portage but it was well worth it. We saw a lot of moose tracks, and even one or two partridges on the trail in front of us.

We came to a creek that led into the lake and we stopped and rigged up our fly lines. I decided to use a fly rod and a small fly that had been given to me by an old guide in Maine. I had a whole bunch of them tied up in size sixes and tens, and we would take turns, one guy would paddle and the other guy would troll with a fly line with this wonderful fly on the end of it. We caught one trout after the other. They all ran sixteen to eighteen inches, some maybe even twenty inches. They were the most beautifully colored fish. I think that a brook trout—or a speckled trout as they call them in Canada—fresh out of the water, is one of nature's most spectacular fish. We probably caught sixty or seventy trout that day between us and we turned them all back in the water except three.

Later in the afternoon, we went up on shore and cleaned the three trout and had a shore lunch. I scurried around in the woods until I found a big slab of bark, and I filleted the three fish, and pinned the fillets to the bark with some pointed sticks that I sharpened with my knife. We built a fire and set this piece of bark up alongside the fire, and broiled those fish. We put salt and pepper on them, and with the rest of the lunch we had, it was a fantastic treat. Just to sit there in that wilderness, eating that wonderful trout fillet, was quite a wilderness experience for both of us.

When we got through with our meal and started back home, we had that same long carry over the portage and the game trail. We put the canoe in the lake, and damned if we didn't have the same bunch of otters follow us all the way back down the lake again. My guest kept taking picture after picture all day long. He must have taken a hundred pictures of the otters, the loons, the bear, and all the other things we did that day. We got back to the lodge, sat there in front of the fireplace and talked about the trip.

My guest said, "John, of all the trips I've ever had, this one today was one of the most enjoyable. It was fantastic." I thought so as well.

I would handle a few moose hunters each fall up at my lodge. I always went up myself in late fall to see that the hunters had everything they needed. I would go to Blind River, pick up two or three guides, bring them back, and put them in the guide's cabin at the lodge. They would stay at the lodge for the whole moose season until they finished hunting.

Along with the lodge, I had what they called an outpost cabin. It was a cabin that was built back in the woods on another lake. It was quite a drive and a long canoe trip to get to it. It was very isolated and in a really wild part of the country, but it was in good game and fishing country. I would leave the door on this outpost cabin unlocked. I had it furnished and stocked with food in tin cans to keep the mice from eating the food. I would leave a sign on the door that whoever wanted to use it was welcome, but they had to keep it clean and replace whatever wood they used for the fireplace. A lot of people—travelers, hunters, and Indians—would stop in that cabin overnight and would always leave some kind of note of thanks.

The time I owned that lodge was wonderful for me. I had my own cabin up there, and I always had friends visiting me. We always had a good time. I regretted letting go of it in one way, but as I said, you can spread yourself too thin.

20

Sportsmanship And All That

I have been a sportsman and an outdoorsman all my life. I have tried to follow the good principles of sportsmanship in all my hunting and fishing, and deplore those individuals who have done otherwise. I have seen a number of them, and they do no credit to themselves, and only bring a bad name to those of us who really care about the future of hunting and fishing. I have hunted a lot and I have killed my share of game animals and taken my share of fish. But this was nature's bounty and I did it always with a profound respect for the ways of nature.

I have seen hunters that have never sighted their rifles before going hunting, whether it was for moose or for deer or for any other game. I have seen them put their rifles away after hunting season and never look at them again until they take them out the next season. They have no idea whatsoever whether they are going to hit the target. They don't know whether their scope is knocked out of shape or line or anything else. To me, these are poor and inconsiderate hunters who bring a bad name to the sport of hunting.

But, there are worse. Those are the selfish cheats who will do almost anything to get an animal or fish, and ignore almost every principle of sportsmanship. I have been on a number of hunting and fishing expeditions with some of them and I would never go a second time with them.

I remember one fellow in particular whose sportsmanship was terrible. I went mule deer hunting out west with him one year. We had all killed our deer and antelope and this guy took his .22 rifle and went back out on the prairie.

I heard him plinking away at something and wondered what he was up to. I walked back to him and there he was sitting on top of a hill shooting at antelope. I asked him, "What the hell are you doing?"

"Trying to see if I can kill an antelope with this .22," he said.

"My God, man, can't you see," I said, "That you're just wounding them. After you hit them, they're just running away, and you'll never be able to catch them and put them out of their suffering?"

"Yeah," he said. "But this is damn good target practice."

I called him every name I could think of and a few more besides. I told him what kind of an SOB he was, and that I would never hunt with him again. It was a promise I kept.

I remember another individual from East Lansing who was very prominent. He took films of all his hunting trips to Canada, and delighted in showing them to his friends. He gave me some to watch, and the only thing I was impressed with was his poor sportsmanship.

One film he had was entirely about hunting wolves in Canada from an airplane. They used a Piper Cub with two guys in it. They had a pilot up front and a guy sitting in back with a shotgun. They would fly out over back country lakes, and find a wolf pack with maybe six or ten wolves out on the open ice, a mile or two from shore. Then they would fly over them and shoot the wolves out of the side of the airplane.

Many times they would just wound the wolves or knock them down. The wolves would lie there flopping around. They had skis on the airplane so they could land on the lake. Then they would get out and finish killing the wolves. The animals never had a chance to get away from that airplane. I often wondered whether the Canadian government knew about that way of killing wolves.

They took pictures of the hunters with their kill along side the aircraft. They would lift the jaws of the wolves open to show the teeth and the poor animals would be all shot to pieces from the shotgun blast and bloody from head to foot. It was a very gory sight.

Another film he had was on how he hunted moose in Canada. He used a helicopter and set up a hunter in the back with a high powered rifle. When they spotted a moose, they would fly over the treetops and run him almost to death. When they got close enough for a killing shot, the hunter would shoot the moose directly from the helicopter. Then they would lower someone down in a sling. He would put a line on the moose, and they would pull both the guy and the moose up to the helicopter and fly back to camp. The animals never had a chance. It was a pitiful thing to see this on film. On this one trip, I bet he had ten moose stacked up on that dock. Such sportsmanship is terrible.

I have been in some northern towns in Michigan during deer hunting season, where people were selling deer killed before the season began for thirty or forty dollars apiece. All you had to do was check around, and you could find some guy who would have a barn full of deer, as many as forty or fifty hanging from the rafters. You could pick out just about any sized deer you wanted.

I have been on many trips that have been completely ruined because of the selfishness and the unsportsmanlike conduct of some of the people that were in the party. And I have had some real brawls about it with some of them. Some took offense at being criticized. They said they paid a big license fee, and paying a lot of money entitled them to the game any damn way they wanted. They got their game, but they didn't go with me a second time.

I have taken some of my frustration out on poor hunters and poor sportsmen, and I would like to conclude with a funny story I heard about deer hunting in Michigan.

It seems there were two guys that went deer hunting together in northern Michigan every year. They never got a deer and never brought any venison home. One year they went up, and their wives decided to drive up where they were and find out what was going on. They drove to the house where the two guys were staying and knocked on the door. A woman came to the door and asked them what they wanted.

"We're looking for John and Joe So and So," they said.

The woman at the door said, "They're not here. I made lunches for them this morning and they're out hunting."

"Oh," the two wives said. "Thank you so much." So they left.

In the car, they looked at each other and said, "Well, we must be wrong. We thought those guys were up to something. But, I guess they're not. They're just having bad luck. Maybe we better turn around and go back home."

"Well," one wife said, "Let's wait another day and we'll

check again tomorrow. If it's the same thing, we'll just leave and never tell them we came up here."

So they waited until the next day. They went over to the house again and knocked on the door. The same woman came to the door again. Again, they asked if John and Joe So and So were there.

The woman put her hands on her hips and said, "Why don't you two prostitutes leave these guys alone. They brought their wives up with them this year, and they don't want to be bothered by the likes of you."

21

Tales Of A Canoe

This is a story about canoes and the joy of owning one. I have owned many canoes in my life, some good and some bad. I have traveled hundreds of miles in a canoe paddling along leisurely, watching and listening, and looking at the woods and the rivers.

Few people will ever love the woods and waters and the trout streams the way I have in the eighty-five years that the good Lord has blessed me.

The one canoe that stands out in my mind is a gorgeous wood Peterboro canoe that I owned back in 1935. It was a live thing to paddle, and it always seemed to know when we were going on a trip. It had an urge to go and a way to go that was just like a living thing.

I loved that canoe very much but I can't remember what happened to it. It was one of the best made and best handling canoes I ever had.

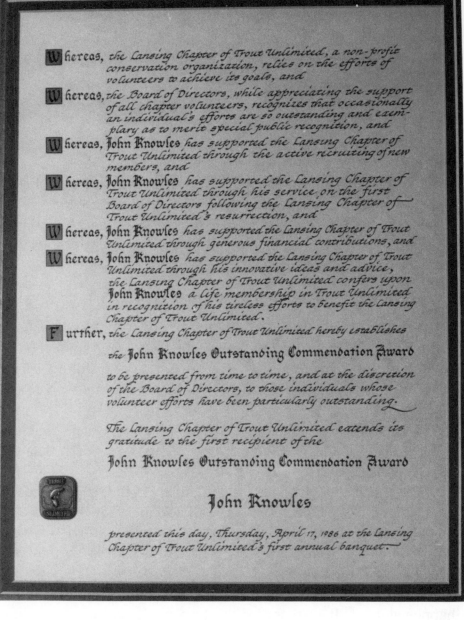

Whereas, the Lansing Chapter of Trout Unlimited, a non-profit conservation organization, relies on the efforts of volunteers to achieve its goals, and

Whereas, the Board of Directors, while appreciating the support of all chapter volunteers, recognizes that occasionally an individual's efforts are so outstanding and exemplary as to merit special public recognition, and

Whereas, John Knowles has supported the Lansing Chapter of Trout Unlimited through the active recruiting of new members, and

Whereas, John Knowles has supported the Lansing Chapter of Trout Unlimited through his service on the first Board of Directors following the Lansing Chapter of Trout Unlimited's resurrection, and

Whereas, John Knowles has supported the Lansing Chapter of Trout Unlimited through generous financial contributions, and

Whereas, John Knowles has supported the Lansing Chapter of Trout Unlimited through his innovative ideas and advice, the Lansing Chapter of Trout Unlimited confers upon John Knowles a life membership in Trout Unlimited in recognition of his tireless efforts to benefit the Lansing Chapter of Trout Unlimited.

Further, the Lansing Chapter of Trout Unlimited hereby establishes

the John Knowles Outstanding Commendation Award

to be presented from time to time, and at the discretion of the Board of Directors, to those individuals whose volunteer efforts have been particularly outstanding.

The Lansing Chapter of Trout Unlimited extends its gratitude to the first recipient of the

John Knowles Outstanding Commendation Award

John Knowles

presented this day, Thursday, April 17, 1986 at the Lansing Chapter of Trout Unlimited's first annual banquet.

Trout Unlimited's "John Knowles Outstanding Commendation Award"

The difference between wooden and fiberglass canoes is like the difference in fishing rods. It is like comparing a good cane rod to a glass or a boron rod today. There is absolutely no comparison between them. A cane rod is so much superior and the same with a wooden canoe. A wood hand-made canoe by Peterboro is an outstanding thing to own. If you ever owned one, you'd never forget it for the rest of your life.

In those early days of the 1930's, there were several streams and lakes and rivers to canoe on. I found a host of these places in the upper peninsula of Michigan and in Canada, and the canoe was always my gateway to adventure and freedom.

I loved to leisurely paddle between carries, and to sit and drift, and look and listen like all wild creatures in the woods do. Animals spend most of their time doing just the same thing. To hear the cry of a loon, and to be able to absorb the sounds and the silence, has always been a joy to me that I can't explain in words.

Back in those days, I took a lot of canoe trips. It seems I was always going some place with a canoe on my car. I carried a small backpack and a pup tent with me. I would paddle for a day, fish a little, sit and drift, look and listen to the sounds of the forest, and there was always a new adventure just around the next bend of the river.

One year, my wife and I went on a fishing trip in Canada somewhere up in the French River area for a two week vacation. We traveled only on back roads and trails, trying to keep as far away from civilization as we could. We came around a bend of a trail one day, and there was an Indian who had set up camp. He was building a birch bark canoe around a form of stakes he had driven into the ground right alongside the road. He had almost finished it when we got there.

I stopped and camped across from him. We stayed there two

days just to watch him at work. He was a most meticulous craftsman. He made that canoe right there by the side of the trail with material completely from the woods around him. It was a beautiful thing.

I asked him what he was going to do with it and he said, "Sell it." He offered it to me for seventy-five dollars. Back in those days, seventy-five dollars was a lot of money, and if I had purchased it, I doubt whether I would have had enough money to buy gas to get back home. I was on a real tight budget, and I had to resist the desire to own that canoe and have regretted it all my life. I turned down his offer to buy it, and the thoughts of that canoe have been with me all my years since then.

I can remember him boiling the pine pitch in a tin can, and pressing that in the different edges of the birch bark to make it waterproof. The canoe actually should have been in a museum. It was that good. It was like a picture of an Indian two hundred years ago paddling a beautiful stream in his birch bark canoe.

That canoe today would be a real treasure. I don't even know if it would float but it was about twelve foot long, and the Indian assured me it would be a good canoe in every way.

I have never paddled a real birch bark canoe, and I'll bet that would really have been something to try out. I have many regrets about the opportunity that I missed, and there isn't a thing I can do about it now but think back and treasure those memories.

I can see clearly that the wonderful canoe country is getting farther and farther away every year. Unless we do something now about it, there will come a day when there will be no more wilderness for us to enjoy. We must watch these resources of ours and protect them. We must protect our wilderness as a place to return to, a place to contemplate and restore our souls.

Canoeing is a wonderful way to contemplate and get things

straight in your mind. One night at the end of a portage in Canada, I set up my little pup tent and built a fire. There was a large area of wood ashes from the countless hunters, fishermen, and Indians who had built fires in the same place at this canoe carry.

I picked up a stick and sat there at the edge of my fire. I was poking around in the fire when I saw something odd in the ashes. I picked it up and found an old white clay pipe with a long curved stem.

I was excited about that old pipe and held it in my hands. It must have been a couple of hundred years old. I sat there dreaming of who had last held it, what type of man he was, and how he ever came to lose his treasured pipe in that fire. I tried to picture how he had looked—whether he had been a voyageur or a trapper or just a woodsman. It was a wonderful thing to sit there and hold that pipe and dream like that.

That night when I finally turned in, I heard the chansons of the voyageurs on the river clearly, distinctly and beautiful beyond words. I heard French voices singing and laughing, and the distinct splash of paddles right in front of my tent, but there was absolutely no sign of anybody on the river—no canoes, no people. I heard them come down that stream and pass my tent and go on downstream gradually getting fainter and fainter.

The next morning I wondered if I had dreamed the whole thing. Then I thought that in this wonderful age of technology that maybe, just maybe, we are going at too fast a pace and perhaps the old ways were better. Before I left the portage that morning, I took the old clay pipe out of my pack and just sat there and looked at it. As I held it, I felt a distinct feeling of electricity that tingled the palm of my hand. I sat there for a long time and just wondered.

Now as I look back over my life, I truly feel that I have

been blessed. I have been blessed with good health and a long life, and I have had the opportunity to enjoy so many wonderful things in the outdoors—adventures that very few people have had the opportunity to enjoy. I have enjoyed every moment of it, every incident, every friendship, every excursion and every adventure that I have had. No one could ask for more. I am happy.